THE ULTIMATE BETRAYAL

THE ENABLING MOTHER, INCEST AND SEXUAL ABUSE

S0-CFO-512

AUDREY RICKER, PhD

SEE SHARP PRESS • TUCSON, ARIZONA

For information contact

    See Sharp Press
    P.O. Box 1731
    Tucson, AZ 85702-1731

Or go to our web site: www.seesharppress.com

Ricker, Audrey.
    The ultimate betrayal : the enabling mother, incest and sexual
abuse / by Audrey Ricker. - Tucson, Ariz. : See Sharp Press, 2006.
    Includes bibliographical references.
    ISBN 1-884365-40-X

    1. Incest victims - Case studies. 2. Child abuse - Psychological aspects -
Case studies. 3. Family psychotherapy

616.85836

Cover design by Kay Sather. Interior design by Chaz Bufe.

CONTENTS

PART III – Present and Future

INTRODUCTION

The uproar about "stranger danger" and Internet predators diverts attention from the real child abuse problem: over 80% of child abuse happens within the family. Statistics tell us that at least one in every six children in our country will be sexually abused before they leave childhood.[1] Yet we cannot bring ourselves to talk about the parents who directly participate in or enable the sexual abuse of their own children.

Millions of children are sexually abused by one or more of their own family members, usually with the knowledge and consent of other family members. Yet we rarely talk about this. If this were any other problem even remotely as serious and widespread, it's certain that we would hear about it—loudly and repeatedly.

The Ultimate Betrayal opens with what one would hope would be the normal response by a mother to the abuse of her children: outrage followed by action against the perpetrator. Unfortunately, this response isn't the norm. Enabling behavior is more common—behavior in which the mother ignores the abuse or even actively aids the perpetrator.

That behavior, and its effects, is the subject of this book; and it's one of the last taboos in our culture. This book will likely be shocking and upsetting to readers who have only experienced nurturing, caring mothers. However, this book will provide relief and validation to those who have seen dysfunctional mothers through their work in the legal system or as therapists—or as the child of an enabling mother.

Whether you work as a prosecutor or counselor, or are an abuse survivor, we hope that you will find a deeper understanding of the dynamics of the abusive family through the following:

The Role of the Mother in Child Abuse

The U.S. Department of Health and Human Services (DHHS) comprehensive survey of child maltreatment in 2004 reports that, "Approximately 40 percent of child victims were maltreated solely by their mothers; another 17 percent were maltreated solely by their fathers; 19 percent were abused by both parents, 7 percent were abused by the mother and another person. Other relatives of the child were the perpetrators 5 percent of the time. Child victims abused by non-familial perpetrators accounted for only 11 percent of the total."

While these statistics encompass all forms of child maltreatment, it is significant that the mother, at 40%, is the predominant source of mistreatment of children. When one includes the 19% of abuse incidents in which both parents participated, and the 7% in which the mother and another person hurt the child, the amount of abuse in which the mother participated jumps to 66%. And almost 90% of child maltreatment is caused by a family member. In contrast, all non-family members are responsible for only 11% of child maltreatment. Thus, it appears that the leading source of danger to a child is his or her parents.

While the Department of Health and Human Services report encompasses all kinds of child maltreatment, similar percentages appear in two smaller studies of child sexual abuse perpetrators. These studies identify 80% of perpetrators as interfamilial, with only 20% of perpetrators coming from outside the family.[2]

These studies only refer to direct abuse. If one also considers participation in enabling activities as abuse, the percentage of parent participation in child abuse rises even higher.

The correlation between domestic violence and childhood sexual abuse

"The most significant predictor of whether a battered woman will physically abuse her child is having been physically abused by her own mother–not being battered by her partner."[3]

"75% of child rape was related to histories of physical abuse." "Women who were sexually abused are three times at higher risk for later domestic violence. . . . Predictors of later domestic violence histories include Child Sexual Abuse, emotional abuse, alcohol abuse, and a low educational level. . . . Severity of Child Sexual Abuse is the strongest predictor of later victimization in intimate partner violence."[4]

These quotations from studies indicate that domestic violence is a predictor or precursor of child sexual abuse, and that child sexual abuse is a precursor or predictor of domestic violence. It's a chicken-or-the-egg situation. Whether you are in law enforcement, the judicial system, child welfare, or family counseling, anecdotal evidence in your field has long suggested that abuse runs in families and continues through the generations. Now research supports the validity of those observations. Whether the mother is the perpetrator of domestic violence, or victim, or both perpetrator and victim, her role in domestic violence profoundly affects the future of her children.

Childhood Sexual Abuse and the Dysfunctional Family

"Studies have not found differences in the prevalence of child sexual abuse among different social classes or races. However, parental inadequacy, unavailability, conflict and a poor parent-child relationship are among characteristics that distinguish children at risk of being sexually abused."[5]

There is no correlation between socio-economic status or race with childhood sexual abuse. It is family dysfunction that puts children at risk. To better understand the dynamic of dysfunctional parents and how their parenting styles put their children at risk, we turn to the work of Dr. Kalyani Gopal, researcher, therapist and teacher. In over 25 years of working in the field of child sexual abuse, Dr. Gopal has developed a model she describes in her upcoming book, *Toxic Parenting Styles*.

Here are Dr. Gopal's four Toxic Parenting Styles[6]:

1) Guardian-oriented parenting style
- Overindulgence
- Overprotection
- Infantilization
- Hypervilgilance
- Pity
- Excessive concern
- Lack of independence
- Enmeshed relationship with child
- Seen in families with sick children

2) Exploitation-oriented parenting style
- Verbal abuse
- Physical abuse
- Neglect

- Emotional abuse
- Dejuvenilization
- Sexual abuse

3) Abuse-oriented parenting style

- Difficulty showing affection to children
- Poor sense of identity
- Overprotective/neglectful
- Insecure, preoccupied, forgetful
- Boundaries struggles
- Passivity, envy of child's normalcy
- Unrealistic developmental expectations
- Role reversal
- Somatization
- Seen in families with histories of abuse
- Parentified child

4) Victim-oriented parenting style

- Helplessness
- Child becomes the caretaker
- Child fearful of parent hurting/killing self
- Role reversal
- Threatened by child's need for independence
- Actions of self-injury to keep child in caretaking role
- Whiny, complaining, condescending, cajoling, manipulative style

These descriptions apply to the parents we find in *The Ultimate Betrayal's* case studies. The author argues that dysfunctional parenting facilitates, or enables, the abuse perpetrator. Given how closely the parents in the case studies conform to the above "toxic parenting styles," this certainly seems to be the case.

The *Encyclopedia of Crime and Punishment* states that the betrayal of trust experienced by the child victim, when the parent is the perpetrator, actually aggravates the damage done by sexual abuse. It is usually less traumatic for a child to be victimized by a stranger than by a family member. Not only does the dysfunctional family increase the risk to the child, and increase the psychological damage, but the dysfunctional family also fails to provide the supportive parental relationship that helps the child to recover.

Thus, we have the triple whammy of the dysfunctional family. First, the dysfunctional family puts the child at risk. Second, parental involvement in the abuse aggravates the injury to the child. Third, the lack of functional parenting impedes recovery. This is why understanding the family dynamic in child sexual abuse is so key to protecting the child. And, when we fail to protect the child, understanding the dysfunctional family dynamic is necessary to understanding how to help the child heal.

Childhood sexual abuse as a predictor of subsequent rape

"If the perpetrator of the crime is a parent rather than an adult stranger or older child, the child is more likely to experience distress."[7]

The *Encyclopedia of Crime and Punishment* reports, "[C]hildren are approximately three times more likely to be the victims of rape. In fact, among females, almost 30% of all forcible rapes occur before the age of 11, and another 32% occur between the ages of 11 and 17." And having been raped once increases the probability of a subsequent victimization, especially when the first sexual assault or rape was when the victim was a child.[8]

The family should be the first line of defense for the child. As we have seen, this is too often not the case, and the child pays the price. To stop the violence, "parents should educate their children about appropriate sexual behavior and how to feel comfortable saying no."[9]

But this kind of responsible parenting is not likely to occur in a dysfunctional family. Further, as this book makes clear, in the enabling family not only is the child *not* given protective messages. Instead, the child gets the message that he or she *cannot* say no, or even has the right to say no. It is obvious how this facilitates the perpetrator.

The impact of childhood sexual abuse

The effects of childhood sexual abuse on survivors include: post traumatic stress disorder–30% to 50%; depression and anxiety–over 33%; sexualized behavior–over 30%; promiscuity–38%; general behavior problems–30%; poor self-esteem–35%; and disruptive behavior–23%.[10] In addition, adult victims may turn to substance abuse, self-mutilation and eating disorders.[11]

The trauma of childhood sexual abuse is hard enough. Unfortunately the after effects of sexual abuse create serious secondary traumas. These traumas have serious health effects, relationship effects, and even affect the survivor's ability to function at school and at work. Worse, the people around the survivor may not realize what they are seeing is a symptom of childhood trauma, and may instead blame the victim, making the victim feel yet worse. Survivors may not even realize that behavior they don't understand and may not think they can control is an after-effect of abuse; and many blame themselves for their trauma-induced behaviors.

Approximately 15% to 20% of the adult population in the United States are survivors of childhood sexual abuse. Drug addiction, depression, teen pregnancy, trouble in school, self-mutilation, criminal acts, and eating disorders have all been identified as results of childhood abuse. Yet, only a very small number of abuse survivors realize that there is a connection between the problems they experience as adults and their childhood sexual abuse. Unfortunately, an even smaller percentage of survivors have access to the kind of reparative therapy Audrey Ricker provides in her practice and describes in this book.

Statistics identify correlations. Cause and effect relationships are much harder to establish. As we see from this book's case studies, the effects of childhood sexual abuse live on for decades. But as we also see, no matter how long it has been since the abuse occurred, repair of the damage is possible. *The Ultimate Betrayal* is an excellent self-help tool for survivors and an eye-opening analysis of the role and effects of the enabling parent.

– Katherine Trimm

1. Gopal, Kalyani. *Impact of Sexual Abuse: Children, Adolescents, and Adults.* Nashville, TN: Cross Country Education, 2006, p. 8.

2. Ibid.

3. Coohey, C. "Battered Mothers who Physically Abuse Their Children," *Journal of Interpersonal Violence,* 19 (8) 2004

4. Gopal, op. cit., p. 6.

5. Finkelhor, David. "Current Information on the Scope and Nature of Child Sexual Abuse." *The Future of Children,* 4 (2), 1994.

6. Gopal, Kalyani. *Toxic Parenting Styles.* Not yet published.

7. Dominquez, R. Z., and Nelke, C. F. and Perry, B. D. "Child Sexual Abuse," *Encyclopedia of Crime and Punishment Vol 1.* Thousand Oaks, CA: Sage Publications, 2002.

8. Gopal, "Impact of Sexual Abuse," op. cit., p. 32.

9. "Child Abuse." AHA Fact Sheet #4. Englewood, CO: American Humane Association, 1993.

10. Domingues and Nelke, op. cit.

11. Sgroi, Suzanne. "Stages of Recovery for Adult Survivors of Child Sexual Abuse." *Vulnerable Populations: Sexual Abuse Treatment for Children, Adult Survivors, Offenders, and Persons with Mental Retardation, Volume 2.* Lexington, MA: Lexington Books, 1989.

A Therapist's Comment

In the study of sexual abuse and sexual assault of women, analysis has focused overwhelmingly on the role of males. Analysis has emphasized how the treatment of daughters by their fathers has affected the daughters' mental health. There has been very little attention paid to mothers and how they may negatively affect their daughters' psychological development. By ignoring the mother/daughterdynamic and its long-term impact, I believe we do a disservice to all family members.

It is unpopular to explore the role of a victim's parents, especially the mother, in a child's sexual trauma (whether it is childhood abuse or sexual assault at a later age). "Blaming" a parent, especially the mother, for the abuse perpetrated by another individual is stigmatized. This book, however, is not about blame. It is not about finding fault and placing it on someone who is not the perpetrator. The goal here is to learn about ourselves, our roles, and how we can attempt to heal and reduce the occurrence of abuse in future generations.

From the beginning of time human beings have venerated the mother/child bond. Most of us, Christian or not, have no difficulty conjuring up the image of the Virgin Mary cradling her infant while a warm glow surrounds them. We have received the message that the relationship between mother and child is sacred, pure, and perfect. To question or challenge this relationship is not only frowned upon, but may be viewed as blasphemous. Be that as it may, reality intrudes. As a psychotherapist I have not been able to ignore the difficulties my clients have experienced as a result of their relationships with their mothers.

I have worked with countless sexual abuse and sexual assault cases. Initially, the focus is on the crisis at hand and helping the client get through this difficult time. During the initial visits, the mother of a victim will sometimes accompany the victim to a session, presenting herself as a supportive ally who is there to emphasize where the blame needs to be placed. Unfortunately, there is usually little room during this time of crisis to explore issues of long-term family dynamics. Some clients, however, do continue the therapeutic process beyond dealing with the incident which brought them in. It is in this further exploration that the pieces of the puzzle begin to come together.

As the therapy deepens, it becomes evident that complex and deep-seated family issues underly the sexual trauma lie complex. These issues often involve the client's relationship with her mother.

There are cases where the mother has been overtly abusive or neglectful, and with work the client becomes able to identify the situations in which her mother treated her in abusive ways. The more difficult cases include mothers who have smothered their daughters with their own needs, subtly encouraging caretaking by the daughters. These are mothers who have been, and often still are, controlling, intrusive and narcissistic, mothers who have used their daughters for their own ends, sometimes living vicariously through them without realizing it. Often, these mothers appear extremely helpful and loving. However, what remains hidden is the intense and long-term damage these mothers have done to their daughters. This covert mistreatment is hard to deal with, because it is difficult for the client to identify it.

But the results of overt and covert abuse are the same: low self-esteem, low self-worth, lack of boundaries, lack of self-identity, and intimacy issues, just to name a few of the more common problems. These difficulties often contribute to sexual abuse and sexual assault.

The Ultimate Betrayal brings these important issues to the fore. It explores in depth the dynamics between mother and daughter, and discusses how mother-daughter difficulties have come about, and what role they have played in the victim's life. Audrey Ricker brings a wealth of knowledge and experience to this discussion. Her book is an invaluable resource for both practitioner and victim. The more we honestly explore these issues, the more clarity we will have, and the more easily we will heal ourselves (or help heal our clients).

– Ophelia Zamora, licensed psychotherapist and sexual abuse therapist

FOREWORD

During my career as a criminal prosecutor, I was struck by the pattern of abuse that seems to run in families, generation upon generation. There were, of course, "bad families" whose repeated run-ins with the law made up a significant part of my case load. But then there were a relatively small number of families who provided a disturbing number of the victims of sexual assault, sexual conduct with a minor, and incest. I used to wonder what special kind of radar the perpetrators used to identify their victims. After reading this book, I now know that there is no special radar. The perpetrators read the signs we refuse to acknowledge.

As an assistant d.a., I saw perpetrators of sexual assault avoid prosecution because law enforcement and prosecutors perceived the victims as "problematic": the victims dressed provocatively or used drugs, or the family members denied that the assault ever occurred. Some families even claimed that thirteen- or fourteen-year-old children were having consensual sex with men in their twenties. Why so many victims were "problematic" was a mystery to me and many other prosecutors.

Now, at last, we have a fascinating, clear-eyed look at the family dynamics that can keep the survivors of incest/sexual assault stuck in victimhood. In *The Ultimate Betrayal*, Audrey Ricker has provided a valuable tool for evaluating the behaviors and family dynamics that deliver victims to perpetrators. *The Ultimate Betrayal* is a useful self-help guide for victims and a valuable resource for counselors.

The point of Audrey's book is not to blame the mother and leave it at that. Audrey provides a framework within which the victim can analyze the feelings and circumstances surrounding the incest/sexual assault, recognize the vulnerabilities that the perp took advantage of, and then learn to overcome the emotional damage caused by the abuse. Audrey has produced a highly readable book, infused with hope and the unflagging belief that facing the role that mothers play in incest and sexual assault is essential in guiding victims to survival.

– Sue Supp, attorney at law, former Pima County assistant district attorney

PREFACE

When I began treating clients who had survived incest, sexual assault and/or sexual molestation, I believed that the mothers of victims would be like Moira, a friend who works at the local university. When Moira found out that her ex-husband had molested both of her teenage daughters for over a year, she began immediate individual and group treatment for the girls, as well as for herself, so she could deal with her guilt and rage, and know how to assist in her daughters' recovery. Since the abuse happened on weekend visits with her ex-husband, and he had threatened to harm her daughters and Moira if they told, Moira could not have known what was going on. Still, she is consumed by self-blame. Somehow, she tells herself, her friends, and her therapist, she should have figured it out, she should have seen clues.

She blames herself even though she did not rest in her attempts to see justice done. Her fight to have her ex-husband incarcerated took several years and all her savings, but it finally succeeded. He was sentenced to 20 years in prison.

But the mothers of my clients did not react to the knowledge of their children's incest as Moira had. These mothers proved to be so different from what I expected—yet so similar to one another in so many ways—that I decided to write about them and their behaviors.

I first became interested in the mothers of my clients when, by mistake, I wrote a description of one client's mother in another client's progress notes and realized that, except for a few details, the description did not need to be changed. These mothers' behaviors, attitudes, and harmful effects on my clients were almost identical. I then read the progress notes of my eighteen other clients and saw that, with the exception of two rape victims, they all had essentially the same mother.

This mother's role in the drama of abuse and/or incest and/or molestation—that of enabler—is as crucial as the perpetrator's, and consists of four basic tasks: 1) refusing to interfere with the incest—for instance, by pretending to be asleep when the father gets up and leaves the bedroom at night; staying out of the house on errands during certain times of the day; not disturbing the perpetrator and victim when they go into a room and shut the door; 2) discouraging the victim from hating the perpetrator by pretending that the family is perfect and that the father is performing his paternal duties well; 3) suggesting that the victim deserves the abuse by giving her the unspoken but clear message that she is a temptress who is inherently bad; 4) making the victim need attention from the abuser by denying her the maternal love, validation, and soothing every child needs.

All of the mothers of my clients who experienced incest, as well as sexual molestation and assault, as children, performed these four tasks. These mothers' destructive impacts on the victims' lives did not stop when the incest stopped. These mothers continued to adversely affect the victims' feelings about themselves, their choices of mates, and their living situations; and they would have continued to do so if the victims had not sought therapy relating to incest, assault, and molestation.

My clients are not the only survivors of sexual abuse, incest, and molestation to have such mothers. In her book, *Memory Slips*, concert pianist Linda Cutting describes her mother as carrying out all four enabling tasks. Her mother pretended not to know when her husband came to her daughter's room at night; she insisted that since the father was a minister he could do no wrong; she made all family members keep up the façade of the perfect family even after the author's two brothers committed suicide; and, except for very rare motherly incidents, she denied her daughter unconditional motherly love. This mother eventually cut all ties when her daughter reported the father's abuse to the Methodist clergy (which apparently did not affect his career adversely in any way). In her autobiography, *Second Seduction*, Frances Lear (best known for being the editor of the glossy woman's magazine, *Lear's*, and the ex-wife of television producer Norman Lear) said that her coldly indifferent mother knew very well what her stepfather was doing when he left their bedroom every night for 30 to 45 minutes.

The mother's role in incest sometimes continues after the survivor grows into an adult no longer vulnerable to sexual victimization.

Clients sometimes find that their mothers have set up their children —and sometimes grandchildren—for incest, molestation, and assault either by the perpetrator or by other people with whom the mother has become involved. This situation existed with four of my clients, and possibly three others.

Eventually, as my practice grew, I was able to identify the common characteristics that kept cropping up over and over again in clients' descriptions of the mothers involved in incest, sexual assault, and molestation:

- Matriarchal status in the family;
- Control of the victim's feelings;
- The ability to create fierce loyalty among all her children;
- The ability to control and destroy the victim's self-esteem;
- The ability to alienate the victim emotionally;
- An unexplained dislike for, and scapegoating of, the victim;
- Resilience that allows this mother to pursue a successful career, as well as relationships with other children and new partners, if she divorces, while in many cases the victim remains devastated, in need of psychiatric medication, unable to tolerate relationships with anyone, or even to live independently;
- The belief that she is a good parent because of the gifts, visits, or other parenting gestures she bestows on her other children and even, now and then, on the victim;
- The belief that she has the power to designate a child as prey.

I found these characteristics and behaviors so often in my clients' mothers that I became alarmed. Was I creating this mother out of too few clues? Was I trying to blame the mother figure for all of my clients' problems? Was I projecting my attitudes onto the clients' mothers? I finally decided that whatever the reasons for my perceptions, the facts spoke for themselves.

After careful self-examination, I realized that I had not invented this enabling mother in my therapy work. I had instead seen her emerge, unsolicited, from my clients' descriptions of their incest, molestation, and/or abuse in childhood.

In my first weeks of work as a therapist in the sexual incest/assault field, I encouraged clients to express anger at their perpetrators. But my clients never seemed to work through their anger. They would keep re-expressing it in routine ways that seemed exhausting, but also somewhat boring to them. Those clients who had been in therapy previously told me that they had expressed their rage at their perpetrators so often that the rage no longer meant anything to them. Those clients who had more than one perpetrator would find themselves not knowing which perp to hate most on which day.

Then Norice came for therapy. A gracious woman in her mid-thirties who suffered such post-traumatic stress disorder (PTSD) symptoms as nightmares, constant crying, and panic attacks, Norice told me longingly how much she loved, and wanted to visit, her mother. Earlier in the session, she had disclosed that the same mother she now longed for had begun selling her and her sisters to male relatives and pedophiles for drug money when the little girls were four, five, and seven years old. I found myself interrupting her declaration of love for her mother. "Excuse me," I said, cutting short Norice's expression of mother love. "I need to tell you something." I took a deep breath. "I am feeling a lot of anger for your mother on your behalf. I can't help it." I took another deep breath. Norice stared at me, as though stunned.

"How do you feel when I say that?" I asked. Norice did not answer and continued staring for about 30 seconds. Then her face crumpled and she started crying slowly with long, deep sobs that gradually gathered speed and volume and went on for about 20 minutes. "How could my mother do that to us," Norice wailed when she was finally able to speak. "We were so little and it hurt so much."

The therapy process had begun with Norice and has continued ever since. After that session, Norice told me that she stopped crying at home, became able to sleep through the night without "those awful dreams," and felt "friendlier" toward her children and dog. She is now able to have loving contact with her mother without letting her mother take advantage of her, is handling problems with her children, considering a separation from an unfaithful husband, and is enjoying the sense, for the first time, that she has options in her life. Her symptoms have almost all disappeared.

I then asked other clients to get in touch with their real feelings about their mothers and, with the exception of one who insisted that her mother was not responsible for her incest in any way, got the same therapeutic results. At first, I waited until the third or fourth therapy session to initiate this process. Now I often get to it at the end of the first session. If the client's enmeshment with her mother is not too strong, the client is immediately able to experience her real anger at, and feelings of loss regarding, her mother, and to stop displacing anger onto others. One client who was very enmeshed now struggles with overwhelming feelings of loss, but she is hopeful that she'll "feel better soon—I have to." Sometimes, when holidays come up or new information surfaces, she needs to reprocess her deep feelings about her mother. She experiences longing for her mother again, she must face her anger and loss yet again, and she must let go one more time—but she now knows what is happening and does most of the processing by herself with little help from me.

Other perspectives

I told clients' psychiatrists and case managers about their feelings toward their mothers because I am required to do so by our agency rules. These professionals did not react positively. Two psychiatrists said the clients' siblings would have to corroborate the clients' statements about their mothers before the clients could be believed, and another psychiatrist, who treats two of my clients, said she had met these clients' mothers on several occasions, that she found them perfectly fine, and that she believed the clients were delusional. This psychiatrist said false memories were probably what was "going on here," and that the clients' accounts should not be taken seriously. A social services case manager assured me that her client was "borderline, and you can't believe anything [she] say[s]."

These views were inconsistent with those of my agency, which holds that the client is always to be believed. I had reason to believe these clients anyway, from the way their stories of their childhoods held together under various kinds of questioning. And, I had found that believing the client no matter what was not only greatly appreciated by the client—"You are the first therapist who took me seriously and listened," I heard over and over—but conducive to what seemed to me fairly rapid progress. The hard part for clients—and thus for me—has been processing the loss of the mother once the clients realized their mother's negative impact on just about every aspect of their lives—including their own thoughts and beliefs about themselves and everyone they know.

How this book is organized

The purpose of this book is to help you understand the role of your mother in your incest, molestation, and/or rape, and to deal with the feelings that understanding evokes.

The book is divided into three parts. Part One begins with five simulated therapy sessions. You'll get to answer a lot of the same questions I ask my clients and discover your mother's involvement by analyzing your answers. You'll also find out in this section how to choose a therapist if you are willing to undergo therapy, and how to get the maternal kind of pure-hearted nurturing that everyone needs, now that you know you did not get it, and cannot expect to get it, from your "real" mother.

Part One continues with treatment of the characteristics of mothers who enable incest and sexual abuse of children, with a separate chapter for every characteristic. Incidents from case histories are used as illustrations, but are heavily disguised to preserve clients' privacy.

Part Two deals with the mother's role in the lives of clients who were sexually assaulted as adults. I was surprised to find that these clients' relationships with their mothers often contributed to the sexual assaults.

Part Three provides information on the effects of sexual assault on my clients' lives. I include this because very few survivors seem to be aware that their strange symptoms—recurring nightmares, terror of sex, desire to reject their children, phobias, multiple personalities, and an annoying tendency to be frequently startled, among others– are normal in sexual abuse survivors.

Note: This book uses the feminine pronouns for the victim and the mother and the masculine for the father because those are the gender roles of the clients discussed in this book. In the one case history of a client whose mother was, and still may be, the perpetrator, and whose father played the supportive "mother" role, the gender pronouns are, as would be expected, reversed.

Why some therapists might not want to deal with the mother's role in incest

You may find that a therapist you consult does not want to believe your mother could have had any kind of role in your incest, perhaps because the therapist is a member of a particular school of therapy. At least four schools of therapy see the mother as unfairly victimized herself by mental health practitioners. Let's examine these schools briefly:

The feminist school of psychotherapy

In the 1960s and 1970s, feminists saw the mother as victim in two ways: 1) society expected her to cater completely to her children, never fulfilling her own needs; and 2) the feminists also saw the mother as a victim of mental health practitioners, because she did indeed seem to be getting blamed unjustly by many psychiatrists, psychologists, and psychotherapists for all their patients' problems.

NAMI followers and PSR practitioners

In the 1980s, the National Alliance of the Mentally Ill (NAMI) declared that mental illness was really a brain illness—meaning the patient is perfectly normal, except for an imbalance of some sort in his brain causing him to behave in ways labeled "crazy" by society. NAMI not only rejected the notion that the mother could cause mental illness, but successfully encouraged mothers to assume the role of heroic advocate for children diagnosed with mental illnesses. A new mental health practice emerged, influenced in large part by NAMI's position on mothers: psychosocial rehabilitation (PSR). PSR practitioners actually assume the role of mother surrogates in their determination to see that the client has the social and occupational connections, housing, clothing, education, and "24/7" kinds of emotional supports necessary for independence. Psychotherapy that does not have independence as its main goal for the client is regarded by PSR as a "medical model" strategy intended to keep the client believing he or she is ill. PSR continues to grow in influence.

False memory syndrome

In the late 1980s, a school of therapists emerged which believed patients' problems were due to parental abuse so horrendous that patients could not consciously remember it. In trying to elicit these "hidden" or repressed memories, many of these therapists ended up implanting false memories of childhood sexual abuse, satanic ritual abuse, and practices such as baby murder in patients' minds by means of hypnosis and suggestion. Believing these memories to be real, patients angrily confronted their parents—thus destroying all relationships with their parents and other family members (who denounced the patient for making horrendous accusations against the parents). Upon realizing the damage done to parents, patients, children, grandchildren, and other relatives by these confrontations, many parents and patients began to sue the professionals responsible for them. Eventually, many mental health practitioners were not only denouncing the false memory syndrome, but also claiming that most reports of child sexual abuse and its reputed harm to victims were either false or exaggerated. Thanks to this, many therapists were and still are reluctant to see the perpetrating or the nonparticipating parent as harmful, especially if the patient has a diagnosis of general or severe mental illness.

Patient-as-unreliable-source school

In the 1980s and 1990s, the for-profit mental health industry began practicing what many felt were exploitative behaviors against patients, their insurance companies, and the governmental agencies funding patients who could not pay. Keeping patients hospitalized in psychiatric hospitals until their insurance was used up and subjecting them to strange therapy modes by uncredentialed practitioners were just two of the abuses inflicted on unsuspecting patients. Congressional investigations and lawsuits by all parties harmed—patients, insurers, and government funders—were the inevitable result. This wave of litigation, plus the litigation of the False Memory Syndrome survivors and their wrongly accused family members, led to a new kind of defensive practice by many mental health practitioners: refusal to believe the patients' accounts of what family members did to them unless the reports were corroborated by other family members. Thus, many mental health providers now consider the mother an innocent party wrongly accused by the patient if the patient says she mistreated him in some way. The patient's individual therapy proceeds with the understanding that the patient is "imagining" the parent's mistreatment. This skepticism of the client's/patient's stories until family members have verified them remains common.

A Survivor's Poem

I see lots of creative writing from survivors—poetry, essays, memoirs, jottings. Creative expression helps clients to survive the unbearable. Rather than include a lot of these works, I'm including just one that illustrates the content of this book. The poem "Bring Mom Back" does that in ways that are complex and subtle.

It shows how the survivor of incest, with a mother like those described in this book, feels the need to care and protect the mother despite everything that happened. It also shows how the mother can take everything away from the survivor—not just love, home, her presence in the child's life, and protection from the perpetrator, but the survivor's sense of herself as a person worthy of love.

This poem was written by a 15-year-old girl. At the time she wrote it she was sitting on her aunt's balcony, alone again, "writing and writing and writing" as a way of expressing her feelings.

Bring Mom Back

A drink, a chug, one more swallow
Her troubles will be gone, until tomorrow
She thinks a bottle will take away her mistakes and regrets
Regrets she cannot face. The pills and drink—these are her pets
I love her dearly but cannot see
Why she doesn't believe in me
I've helped her, guarded her
protected her and loved her
If and when he's put away, tell me will this be her cure
My life is unfulfilled without my mother
And those cute pranks from my brother
When her bottle is thrown away and she turns the key
Will it finally bring her
back to loving me

– *Crying Eyes*

PART ONE

CHILDHOOD TRAUMA

1

How Your Mother Treated You

In this section, you will "attend" five therapy sessions that will be as close to visiting a therapist as possible. The only difference is that there will be no therapist present, just you and this book. Please try to conduct your sessions in a private place, sitting upright in a comfortable chair, with a fairly low, soothing light. Have the sessions at the same time of day, with no music playing in the background, and have plenty of tissues on hand. Take a pen and a three-ring binder or steno pad with you to every session for recording your answers. Allow 50 to 60 minutes for every session. (It's okay if you finish before the end of the allotted time.) You can go on reading the rest of the book while you are undergoing the "therapy sessions." In fact, it might be a good idea to do so. But you don't have to.

At every session, follow instructions in a relaxed way. This section is all about you, your feelings, and your needs. Please don't tell yourself what should happen in the sessions or what you should feel or think during and after the sessions.

Session One

The steno pad or three-ring notebook that (preferably) has lined paper in it is especially important in this session. If you don't have one or the other, use paper and something firm to write on. Just be sure that paper and pen are handy so you don't have to hunt for them during the session. Please stop and get these items together now, if you don't already have them. When you return, you can continue. Oh, yes, make sure that your chair is comfortable, but not so comfortable that you can't sit upright with your feet on the floor.

All set? Let's get started.

Hello. Welcome to the therapist's office. I'm so glad you came in today. I know this isn't easy, and I think you're brave for being here.

Please answer the following 26 questions. Say them aloud to yourself slowly, pleasantly, and with real caring. All the questions are drawn from common behaviors of the mothers of incest survivors. All are questions that I ask my clients. Write down your answers. They should consist of Yes, Sort Of, Sometimes and No.

1. Did your abuser tell you not to tell your mother about the abuse?

2. Did you ever wonder how your mother could not have known?

3. Did you ever try to tell your mother?

4. Did your mother give you the sense that she didn't want to know about the abuse?

5. Did your mother induce feelings of guilt when you were with her?

6. Did your mother change the subject when you tried to tell her about anything that mattered to you, such as genuine feelings?

7. Did your mother seem jealous of you in any way?

8. Did your mother seem disconnected from you emotionally?

9. Did your mother seem unavailable to you emotionally?

10. Did you long for your mother's company?

11. Did you long for more of your mother's love?

12. Did your mother ever tell you that she was abused by someone as a child and indicate that it wasn't that big a deal?

13. Did your mother ever seem sexually attracted to you?

14. Did your mother ever seem left out of your family, as though she were someone who did not really belong?

15. Did your mother seem emotionally weak to you?

16. Did your mother seem to be under the spell of the abuser?

17. Did your mother ever leave the abuser, but then go back to him?

18. Did your mother treat you like a little doll, always dressing you up and showing you off?

19. Did your mother ever leave you by yourself overnight, or longer, with your abuser?

20. Did your mother ever give you reason to think that she would leave the family if she knew about the abuse?

21. Did your mother believe that without the abuser in the home there would be no money for food, rent, utilities, and other necessities?

22. Did your mother seem to care more about your siblings than about you?

23. Did your mother seem to care more about a religion or belief system than she did about you?

24. Did your mother seem to feel that you were always intrinsically bad, from birth on?

25. Did your mother minimize your fears, night terrors, phobias, and other similar kinds of symptoms as though they were "all in your mind" and something to be repressed and gotten over?

26. Did your mother usually take someone else's side when you told her about something someone had done to you?

Now that you've answered the questions, think about how you feel. Then, allow yourself to feel all your feelings for about ten minutes. Next, put your supplies away in a secure place, get up, stretch, and go on about your day. Return to your chair tomorrow at as close to the same time as you can. Don't return any sooner. You need this "away time" to process the feelings you might be having now.

Session Two

In this session you'll analyze your answers to the questions in Session One, find out what your answers mean, and handle the feelings of betrayal, rage, and despair you might have as a result of your discoveries.

First, count your Yes, Sometimes, and Sort of answers. Ten or more such answers probably mean your mother was aware of your abuse (or is aware, if it's still going on) and didn't stop it.

How can I say this with such confidence? Simply because I have seen this mother hundreds of times with hundreds of clients. These questions identify the ways she behaves toward the survivor. In some cases, the "mother" is the father or stepfather and the perpetrator is another male relative or the mother herself. But the behaviors are always the same.

Reread your answers. Put stars beside the answers that make you the most angry. Put checkmarks beside those that make you the most sad. Put flowers beside those that make you the most depressed and worthless feeling.

Now, give yourself permission to feel all the feelings you have. Go ahead, cry deep, desperate sobs if you need to. Clench your fists in anger if you are angry. Scream if you are alone and feeling rage.

Please, don't cut yourself, drink alcohol, take a pain pill, or do anything else to alleviate the feelings. Just feel them. Just experience them. Sit quietly and shut your eyes while you feel your feelings. Then, when the storm has passed a bit and you feel like a rag doll washed up on the shore, read on.

What just happened

You let yourself face the unspeakable: Your perpetrator was probably not acting alone. Your mother probably suspected what was going on. She suspected and didn't do anything. She allowed your abuse to continue. All she had to do was follow one hunch, one suspicion, one question about where he went off to at night when he thought she was asleep, where he really took you when he went off with you in the car and insisted she not go along, or why her teenage brother or beloved father was always so eager to babysit. But she didn't check. She turned the other way.

If you confront her, she may swear—swear on a stack of Bibles, weeping piteously—that she never knew a thing. Or she'll tell you coldly that you're making it all up, it never happened, and you're evil for even thinking such a thing. But that's because she didn't and still doesn't want to know.

Your positive answers to the questions in Session One indicate that your mother might not have been connected enough to you to help you. She was not connected enough to intrude where she wasn't wanted. She was not connected enough to care more about what was happening to you than about what would make the perpetrator mad.

Oh, God. You're starting to feel angry all over again. It's okay. Take a deep breath and feel your feelings.

You might feel very sad now. That's because you might be facing another fact. You always suspected that she didn't love you, not the way a mother should. You thought that if you just tried hard enough, did enough, put up with the abuse, and didn't blame it on her, she'd see how wonderful you are. Now you are allowing yourself to realize that might not happen, ever. Why? Why, why, why?

There are many possible reasons. You might remind her of someone she hates; you might not remind her of someone she loves; you might be the person she could never be; you might, for reasons nobody will probably ever know, trigger symptoms in her of what might be bipolar disorder or narcissistic personality disorder, or severe envy of some asset—perhaps beauty or a cheerful personality—that attracts people to you rather than to her.

For now, it's best not to think about her at all. Just feel what you're feeling and remember this: Everything you're feeling is good. It's also permissible and even healthy. So for now, don't think. Just feel. Now put your binder and other supplies away, get up, and go on about your day. Come back tomorrow as near the same time as possible.

Session Three

In this session you will: 1) process your feelings of loss; 2) understand why your realizations about your mother mean a partial loss of this person you need so much; and 3) understand why this loss is so hard to bear.

In this session, you might want to use a tape recorder. If you don't have one, just write. The idea is to get your feelings out in a way that will allow you to later hear or read them. Just answer these questions:

- What are you feeling about your mother?
- What did you feel when the incest started?
- What do you feel right now?
- What was the earliest feeling you can remember about anything?

If you don't feel anything in this session, that's fine. Just go ahead with sessions four and five and read the rest of this book. If intense feelings do arise, be prepared to take a nap, call a friend for help, or just sit quietly after the session for as long as it takes for the feelings to subside.

Your feelings may be awful. That's because they are obliterating to some extent the love you have for your mother. Loss of your love for her means, in one sense, loss of her.

This is a serious loss. A mother is usually the most important person in the world to a child. You will hold on to her no matter what, afraid to feel bad things about her because you can't bear to lose her.

Now you might have very bad feelings about her, indeed. All you can do for now is feel these feelings. Pretty soon they'll become bearable.

Your mother will not seem the same to you—but she can still be there. No, she will not be there for you in the same way she was, because now you'll see her in a different light. If it existed, the loss of unconditional love you felt for her is a real loss.

Session Four

This is an unstructured session. It's for reviewing sections one, two, and three, and feeling whatever you feel. Let your thoughts and feelings go in any direction they take, just write them down or record them.

Session Five

In this session you will: 1) understand that you can still have a relationship with your mother and siblings; 2) understand what to expect if you must keep seeing them.

The realizations you have come to in the first four sessions are devastating. You know now that your mother could have done more, probably far more, to stop the incest or molestation. You have all kinds of feelings about that; hate, anger, rage, grief, sadness, and despair could be just a few of them. You can think to yourself: "These are my feelings. They are justified." You are allowed to think these things.

Do you want to confront your mother? If you do, please, please find a psychotherapist who will help you deal with that process. Please don't try it on your own. Instead, feel the feelings you now have, give yourself permission to feel them, and go on with your life. Your mother can now assume a new position. She can become someone you still might relate to on many superficial levels, but who you keep at an emotional distance and no longer adore in the same way you did. You might now feel separate from your siblings, if they go on adoring your mother in the way that you once did and think that you should still do the same. Having that feeling of separation from your sibs is perfectly fine. Many adults have it, and it allows them all to stay on friendly terms for the rest of their lives.

If you go on adoring your mom in the same way you always did, that's okay, too. You can observe yourself adoring her while still letting yourself have all your new feelings. Here's an example of how that observing can work. Suppose you are at a gathering of your family outdoors. The breeze is blowing, the children are playing happily, and you are looking on as your mom brings out some dish she's famous for. You can enjoy the oohs and aahs she gets from everyone present, and enjoy the happy flush that might come to her face. And you can also feel at peace. That's because you no longer have to fight with yourself, pushing down the unexpected and mysterious rage you often feel at these happy family times. Now you know where the rage comes from. If it should bubble up, you can accept it this time, and even embrace it. And you will experience a sense of freedom and liberation you have never felt before.

Also, you can have:

• All the sessions you want. You don't have to stop at five.

• Whatever feelings *you might* have—no matter what family members say you should feel.

• Help from me finding a psychotherapist. Just e-mail me at audreyricker@yahoo.com. If you don't have an e-mail account, you can write to the publisher of this book and they'll forward your message to me, although this will be slower than e-mail. I'll do my best to find someone in your area who I think will be able to help.

———————

Now, a word about the rest of this book: It's full of case histories about my clients' mothers and their roles in what their perpetrators did to them. Case histories of others are valuable in helping you to understand your own history and to realize that you are not alone. There is also a guilty pleasure in reading case histories, sort of like snooping on someone else's real life, the life kept hidden from public view. This pleasure is normal, natural, and it's perfectly all right to enjoy it. Read on.

2

The Enabling Mother's Matriarchal Status

Among all the characteristics of my clients' mothers, matriarchal status is the most common. By matriarchal status I mean a position in the family resembling that of a queen—acting as a central figure around whom all family members' lives revolve. She is consulted on all decisions from the names of new babies to which home to buy. This mother often provides indispensable services such as babysitting and making loans for the buying of new homes and other items, but her main capital is approval—if she gives approval to anyone, she allows that person to belong in the family. If she withholds approval from anyone, she exiles that person from the family. In the case of survivors of incest and molestation as children, this "outside the family" status means life outside the protective walls of the medieval estate—which is just as terrifyingly hostile and unsupportive to these survivors as it was to the general population in medieval times.

This power to decide who is in and who is out of the family gives the mother undisputed power among both immediate and extended family members and renders her above reproach. She is a magnet to whom family members are drawn on holidays, birthdays, and other celebrations. She is the one consulted before they make plans for such events, and she decides who will inherit what heirlooms, where trips will be made, who will go along on the trips and, perhaps more importantly, who will not. All family members seek her favor, even when they criticize her behavior, appearance, or manners behind her back. Her mate is usually passive, deferring to her wishes. If he is a second or third husband, he may be a kind of toy to whom the mother caters and on whom she lavishes attention.

Among incest survivors' mothers, this matriarchal status is so strong that it cannot be undermined by anything, even knowledge of these mothers' role in the incest. The case of Clara provides a good illustration of this kind of mother.

Clara

Clara's three sisters admitted to Clara at various times that they remembered her abuse during their father's "bathroom sessions" with little Clara (during which little Clara's screams could be heard all over the house) and tried to tell their mother to stop it. But none was ever willing to defy their mother and support Clara openly.

Clara's mother rules over a mansion in a gated neighborhood in a southern state. Clara's father, a successful businessman, made this home possible with his earnings and money inherited from his wealthy Boston family. Clara's five grown siblings, their children and their grandchildren, as well as Clara's aunts and uncles and their families and other far-flung relatives, come to this home paying respect and marking holidays and milestones. Clara's parents take many of them on cruises to various corners of the world. Clara's mother encourages daily e-mail correspondence and phone calls. Only Clara is excluded from these activities and from the family as well—because Clara did two things that were very bad.

The first was to call a family meeting at which she confronted her family about the incest her father perpetrated, and her mother assisted in, from when Clara was three to six years old. Clara organized this meeting when she was in her twenties and beginning to fall apart from PTSD symptoms, because she wanted her family to know what was happening to her and why. At the family meeting, Clara's mother was at first stunned, but then admitted tearfully that she knew and sometimes even helped her husband with anal penetration of Clara. She said she knew it was wrong and was sorry she let it happen, but both she and her husband thought Clara had "problems going to the bathroom" that the anal penetration could cure. Instead of ostracizing this mother, the family members blamed Clara for "bringing up old stuff" just to upset the mother and began to shut Clara out of family life.

A few weeks later, Clara's mother denied that the abuse had ever happened, refused to admit she ever said it had, and life in this family went on as usual—but without Clara. Clara's phone calls, e-mails, and letters to her parents telling of her success in her college courses, her happiness at finding a boyfriend who cares about her, and other things, have all gone unanswered. Clara knows that her mother, the matriarch, will, if she has not already done so, cut her out of the family will.

Clara did the second "bad" thing in my office. She called Child Protective Services when she found out that her father was babysitting her new granddaughter by himself.

CPS sent investigators to talk to the grandfather and Clara's daughter, the mother of Clara's grandchild. Even though CPS never told the father and daughter Clara's name, they knew that she was the one who "stuck CPS on us all," as Clara's daughter put it angrily. Clara's daughter then cut off all contact with Clara and still refuses to let her see her granddaughter today. Clara knew her daughter was likely to make this break with her, because the daughter is receiving large sums of money from Clara's mother on a regular basis. Clara has barely enough money to support herself, and now she has no hope of inheriting more. But she can be reasonably sure that her granddaughter will not be left alone with her (Clara's) father from now on. She knows that her daughter does not want this child to be abused, but will do nothing about it herself.

ENID

Enid's mother is the hub of Enid's large family in a Midwest state. Enid's biological father left the family when Enid was three years old, and her mother remarried a "real handsome rogue" when Enid was four. She promptly gave birth to seven more children whom Enid helped diaper, feed, babysit, and raise for the next 15 years. Meanwhile, her stepfather began molesting Enid from the time she was four. He began by "sitting [her] on his lap and fondling [her] private parts" and progressed to intercourse when Enid was seven. The stepfather stopped the incest when Enid was 12, "probably," as Enid put it, "because I started having my period and could have got pregnant." By then, Enid was so entrenched in her role as matriarch's assistant that she went on "doing for everybody" as a teenager, and even after she grew up and became a nurse. Her entire emotional and social life consisted of answering family calls for assistance with illness, births, deaths, and other occasions in which a helping hand was needed. The needy relative would call Enid's mother, and she would demand that Enid "get myself to wherever it was they wanted me to go. I never said no." Her relatives never paid her expenses, and she never asked them to do so. Only when Enid's PTSD symptoms from the incest caused her to be hospitalized and diagnosed as severely mentally ill (SMI) did she realize that the help she had given her family members so freely would not be reciprocated. "Only my mother called when I went in the hospital, and that was to yell at me that I should stop acting crazy and get myself out of there. None of the others wanted to know how I was doing or if they could help me in any way—even though they knew I was not doing well." When Enid told her mother that the incest was the reason she was ill, her mother replied that Enid was making things up, that her stepfather said she was making it all up, and that she shouldn't talk to her again until she was willing to say that she lied about what her stepfather did.

At present, Enid knows that her family is celebrating three new births without her. Her mother did call once to say Enid might be able to attend one such party if she sent a nice enough gift. "But I still haven't sent one thing to that baby; I just can't give my mother the satisfaction. And you know, that hurts because I love new babies just as much as anyone else."

LARRY

Larry's mother is the matriarch of an academic family abounding with distinguished scholars in history, politics, and the humanities. This mother keeps track of conference schedules and submissions, college applications, lecture circuit appearances, and other academic duties for her professor husband, siblings, and three tenure-track, faculty-member children. She knows which preschools and public and private schools are best for their children and which journals to publish in, and she hosts endless social affairs for the administrators and faculty members of the schools where all of the family members are employed. Larry knows that his father molested his two older brothers from the ages of roughly three to eight, and suspects that he was also molested. When Larry and his brothers confronted their mother at a family meeting about being aware of the incest but not stopping it, she denied that she knew and said she had no idea if Larry was molested or not. And Larry's father refuses to say anything about it.

Larry is not dealing with the feelings he has for his mother, because he doesn't know if he has any. He has been taking very strong psychotropic medications since high school, when he was addicted to self-mutilation and his arms became etched with gnarled scars. Now he has almost no feelings at all. All he has are nightmares of being attacked by strange men and a sense of people living inside him who fight brutally with one another all the time.

These memories and symptoms have been troubling enough to keep Larry from reaching his academic and occupational potential. Unlike the other family members, he had to drop out of college after a year. He does not enjoy his minimum-wage job as an inventory associate in a discount chain store, but finds it is the only kind of work he can do. He avoids questioning his parents because he loves being included in the family and attending family gatherings. His brothers, now married and fathers, have dropped the subject entirely because they need the career assistance their mother provides. But really, Larry has admitted in therapy (which he pursues in the slowly dying hope that it might help him remember what really happened to him in his early childhood), the main reason why he and his brothers stay so connected to their mother is that they need her approval very much. She's always been the "real powerhouse" in the family who "takes really good care of us all."

Other kinds of matriarchs

In a few cases, the matriarch-type mother is kind, caring, and genuinely ignorant of the incest going on in her family. But, intimidated by this mother's power and status, the victim is afraid to reveal the incest for fear of interfering with the power the mother enjoys. This was the case with Staci, who was sexually molested by her grandfather from the age of three to five.

STACI

A pretty woman in her late thirties with a host of physical problems for which doctors can find no cause (a common condition in incest survivors), Staci has spent her adult life in service to her mother. A caring, loving woman who adores her five children and two granddaughters, Staci's mom is also a beauty, an excellent cook and housekeeper, and a fashion plate. Staci cannot say enough good things about her mom. She knows she is a disappointment to her mom because she has not been able to finish college, due to learning disabilities and her physical ailments, and because she has not been able to sustain a relationship with a man. She divorced a very abusive husband after 16 years of a "nightmare" marriage, and since then has been involved with two boyfriends, the first of whom didn't want a serious relationship, and the second of whom is currently working on not abusing her anymore.

Staci's four siblings are all in successful marriages and have advanced degrees, professional jobs, and high incomes, while Staci has no degrees, no profession, and only child support income from her ex-husband.

The abuse took place over the course of three summers during Staci's visits to her grandparents. Staci's grandmother was always out of the house on errands when the incest happened. The grandfather would "keep me home when my grandma went out," Staci recalls. She does not blame her grandmother at all, because "Grandma was the best person in the world. It would have killed her if she knew." It also would have killed Staci's mom if she knew, Staci felt. These fears, her love for her grandmother, and her grandfather's threats that bad things would happen if she told, kept Staci enduring the incest for three years. Why did she go back willingly every summer? "I loved my grandma so much and wanted to be with her. And I always hoped my grandpa wouldn't do that to me anymore."

Staci intuited, probably correctly, that her wonderful mother's world would be upended if her mother knew what Staci's grandfather was doing to her. So, like most incest survivors, little Staci decided early on that the incest was somehow her fault and hid it from everyone. After her grandfather's death, when she was 13, Staci told her mother about the incest on the way home from the funeral. Her mother's response? "I always knew there was something wrong with that man. Mom should never have married him." Then Staci's mother said that she didn't want to talk about it anymore; and she has not done so to this day.

When the grandfather's ghost began appearing to Staci at night, beckoning her to come to him with long, white, bony fingers and an "evil expression, the most evil look you can imagine," Staci did not tell her mother. She called instead on God and was soon visited by the ghost of her deceased grandmother, who said she would protect Staci from the grandfather.

So far, the ghost has kept her promise and now visits Staci often, chatting about Staci's daughters and giving Staci encouragement when she needs it. Staci reports often on these ghostly visits in therapy. The ghost of Staci's grandmother says she will always feel guilty about not knowing the incest was happening, and Staci always assures her, "it's all right, I don't blame you." Nor does Staci blame her matriarch mother, who was so loving and caring that she had to be protected from unpleasant news at all times, even at the cost of her little daughter's safety and emotional health.

ELLEN

There is another kind of matriarch who is best described as a "husband worshipper." Ellen is a victim of this kind of matriarch. When I say "victim," I mean that literally, because Ellen's mother allowed her husband to sexually molest Ellen and her two sisters so that he would stay with her. Thus, Ellen's mother victimized her as clearly as the perpetrator did.

Ellen's mother has been a matriarch in every sense of the word, except for having financial wealth. She had five children, four girls and a boy, so she could get welfare money. All five children had different fathers who were uninvolved in their children's lives. Despite the fact there was never any money, often no food, and all too often no running water or electricity in their home, Ellen and her siblings revered their mother. Ellen said she lived for the times her mother was "cuddly" with her, did her hair, and called her pretty and sweet. She felt deeply ashamed when her teachers asked angrily why her mother allowed her and her sisters to have head lice, come to school in dirty clothes, and be so thin. Ellen explained that her mom had to be gone a lot in the daytime to look for jobs, and at night to go to the clubs to find a man, but her teachers didn't understand.

Ellen said that she and her sisters thought their troubles were over when their mother found a man who would marry her and contribute his income to the family. The mother was obviously in love with this man, and soon put him above the children in her attention and affection. The daughters didn't mind, Ellen said, because they genuinely wanted their mom to be happy. "We all just cared about her so much. If she was happy, we were happy."

From the time Ellen was seven to the time she was 13, her stepfather came to Ellen's room at night and fondled her. She later found out he had done the same with her older sisters. It was only when Ellen realized that her sisters were allowing their children to visit this man and her mother that Ellen developed extreme PTSD symptoms and sought therapy.

Now, Ellen wants the strength to end all contact with her mother if the mother continues to be with this man, but is not sure she'll have the strength to do so. "I just miss my mother so much when I'm away from her. I despise her for what she let this man do to us, but I can't give her up. She holds my life together somehow. All us kids feel the same way about her."

Despite Ellen's progress in reducing her PTSD symptoms, she will probably not be able to give up her mother. Her mother has no intention of giving up the man she married and who molested all of her kids except—one hopes—the two youngest who are still living at home.

The fact that I reported to CPS that Ellen's nieces and nephews might be in danger of being molested gave Ellen courage. But it also gave her enormous anxiety, because she was afraid that her mother would be furious at her when CPS came to investigate her husband.

I have no idea what finally happened to Ellen's mother and stepfather. After Ellen went home to visit and confront her mother, she never came back for therapy.

Did your mother have matriarchal status?

Answer Yes, No, or Sometimes to every question.

1. Does your mother run your family like a dictator?
2. Do family members feel that they have to consult your mother about every decision?
3. Does your mother have to know about everything going on in the family?
4. Does your mother influence the naming of babies born in the family?
5. Do you fear your mother's disapproval of your life?
6. Do you feel that your family was like a corporation and your mother was its president?
7. Do you think that other family members might not always like your mother, but fear her?
8. Do you feel that other family members count on your mother in emergencies?
9. Do you feel that family members have to do what your mother wants in order to get the help from her that they need?
10. Do you feel that individuals in your family are less important to your mother than the well-being of the family itself?

If you answered six or more questions Yes or Sometimes, you can be reasonably sure that your mother has matriarchal status in your family.

3

The Mother's Control of the Survivor's Feelings

The need to control others' feelings is common in varying degrees to all the mothers of almost all of my clients. But it's especially strong in the mothers of the incest survivors. Controlling feelings means just that: not allowing the victim's own feelings about the incest to count, and deciding what the victim will feel—especially about her, the mother. As a result, the victim is afraid to feel anything authentic for fear that her mother won't like it and will be displeased with her—a fate the victim fears worse than death.

Nedda's case shows in detail how this control of feelings is done and what effect it can have on others' lives.

NEDDA

Nedda is a 20 year old with two sons, aged one and four. Her mother's second husband molested her from the time she was 13 until she was 16, when the two were caught *inflagrante delicti* by Nedda's grandmother, who lived next door. When her mother blamed Nedda for the molestation and said that Nedda should get out of the house, Nedda "ran away," lived as a homeless teen, got raped on the streets, and later married an 18 year old by whom she was already pregnant.

Marriage and childbirth caused her mother to want to reconcile with Nedda, which made Nedda very happy. When Nedda's husband left her for another woman four years after they married, Nedda was especially glad that her mother was back in her life.

Then Nedda's four year old told her that his 11-year-old half-brother, the son of her mother and the man who abused Nedda, was behaving in sexually explicit ways with him. Nedda's four year old said the 11 year old was fondling and having oral activities with him, which caused Nedda's ex-husband to call CPS. The CPS social worker assigned to the case told Nedda to go into therapy at our agency, which assigned her to me.

But before any therapy could take place, Nedda announced, with a hard, cold look in her brown eyes, that I had to understand one thing: "You can't say anything bad about my mom. She is not to blame." I found out later that Nedda had said the same thing about her mother to a therapist she had seen at our agency after her rape, five years earlier.

In therapy, I found that Nedda was actually very angry at her mother for siding with her stepfather and for not trying to stop Nedda from leaving home at age 16. But she was not angry with her mother for exposing Nedda's own child to sexual abuse from Nedda's half-brother. Every time Nedda began acknowledging to me that her mother was endangering her child by allowing him to be with this boy, Nedda would stop herself and get angry with me. She would turn on me with an angry stare with narrowed eyes that seemed to say, "I know you're trying to get me to blame my mother." "My mother did the best she could!" Nedda would suddenly yell. "She's always been there for me!" Even when Nedda told me in a later session that she discovered that her mother allowed her half-brother to be alone with both her children, something forbidden by her Child Protective Services caseworker, she refused to "blame" her mother in any way. My job, Nedda let me know, was to tell her how to stop her mother from putting her kids in harm's way while not "hurting my mother's feelings. I could never hurt her, ever." When I told Nedda that I was mandated to call Child Protective Services because she had just told me that minor children might be exposed to possible sexual abuse and that Nedda's mother was violating the rule that the 11 year old not be alone with Nedda's children, Nedda was coldly furious with me. After two more sessions (during which Nedda would deal only with her anger at her husband for leaving her), Nedda stopped coming to therapy.

I know that Nedda loves her children. But I also know that Nedda's feelings are so controlled by her mother that she ignores her worries about her children's safety.

OCTAVIA

Death of the victim's mother need not prevent the mother from controlling the victim's feelings posthumously if there are siblings and other female relatives who take on the mother's role. As Octavia discovered in her thirties, just when she thought her life was "coming together" career wise and relationship wise, she was still being manipulated by her mother posthumously via her older sister, Marcella, who had acted as Octavia's surrogate mother for seven years after their mother passed away.

Octavia was subjected to incest by her grandfather, father, and two uncles, and beaten severely by her mother, from the time she was five until she was 13. A matriarchal figure in the family, Octavia's mother gave her oldest daughter Marcella the attention and approval Octavia craved. The message to Octavia from Marcella, Marcella's oldest daughter Gisele, and from other female relatives was, that if she were "normal" (Octavia had been gay from the time she was a teenager), looked nicer, lost weight, and kept a better house, she would get mom's approval, too.

While living apart from her female relatives in her twenties and early thirties, Octavia made a good life for herself. She finished junior college, got a degree in phlebotomy, and had an enjoyable career in that field for several years. She found loving partners she dated and lived with. She pursued sports of all kinds. But she always had the feeling that she wasn't measuring up, wasn't good enough for her family, and that their opinion of her was the only opinion that counted. Finally, in her mid-thirties, Octavia was "driven by some inner urge" to give up her partner, career, house, and friends, and move back to her hometown. She rented a home in the neighborhood where Marcella and Gisele and her ailing father lived and tried to become a part of her family's life—sharing birthday celebrations, special dinners, vacations, graduations, and other events.

But soon, she found herself being "put down" in subtle ways by these relatives. Nothing she did—for instance, the way she wore her hair or decorated her home—was quite right. Then, Marcella began excluding Octavia from family events. Octavia would find out, for instance, that a relative's birthday party had been held without her and would realize that she had simply not been invited. When Octavia asked Marcella about the reasons for this exclusion, Marcella said the family didn't approve of the way Octavia looked and dressed—meaning, Octavia knew, that they didn't approve of her being gay.

This disapproval triggered Octavia to become severely depressed, begin self-mutilating, and become hospitalized. In the hospital, Octavia did not really care that her new girlfriend, who adored her, visited twice a day. She cared only that Marcella, Gisele, and her other female relatives—none of whom even called, much less visited—were ignoring her.

On being released from the hospital, her social services caseworker referred Octavia to our agency. At first, she had a hard time keeping appointments, because family events always seemed to take precedence. It was Christmastime and Marcella had decided Octavia would be included in holiday festivities, which were numerous and constant. Octavia was always calling from shopping expeditions, tree-trimming parties, and gift-wrapping sessions to say she had to cancel. Unfortunately, she soon incurred her female relatives' disapproval by bringing her partner with her to some family events. Marcella then exiled Octavia from the family's ensuing holiday festivities. Devastated, Octavia began her depression-cutting-hospitalization cycle again.

Octavia was more serious about therapy upon being released from the hospital the second time. And she was on the verge of losing her new partner, who didn't like playing second fiddle to Marcella, Gisele, and the other relatives.

After first telling me she didn't care if her partner left, Octavia realized that she loved her partner deeply. She then understood that Marcella was not only controlling her life, but also her feelings about everyone, including herself, and everything, such as her dress and décor. She also realized that the kind of relationships she had with her relatives were one sided and would never provide the kind of satisfaction and nurturing she got from her partner.

After a lot more work in therapy, Octavia was finally able to get in touch with her deep anger at her mother. Tears of rage flowed as she recalled how her mother would beat her with a branch "she made me cut myself" when she tried to tell her mother what her uncles or other male relatives had done to her. Octavia then realized how completely she had replaced her mother with her sister. She saw that she would never get the approval she craved from Marcella and her other female relatives. And Octavia understood she had something most of them, being unattached widows and divorcees, did not—a basically happy relationship with a partner who was openly in love with her.

But Octavia's struggle continues. When she puts herself first, she feels guilty and afraid, sure that some terrible consequence will be visited upon her. She has to learn all over again in therapy that she can feel her own feelings—without first checking out her feelings with Marcella.

Has your mother controlled your feelings?

Answer every question Yes, No, or Sometimes.

1. Have you ever stopped yourself from having feelings you knew your mother wouldn't like?
2. Has your mother ever wept when you expressed a feeling she didn't like?
3. Has your mother ever gotten very angry when you expressed a feeling she didn't like?
4. Has your mother ever told you that you did not feel something you said you were feeling?
5. Has your mother ever made you feel guilty about your feelings?
6. Has your mother ever told you that what you were feeling was bad, wrong, and/or evil (or unacceptable in some other way)?
7. Have you felt afraid to tell your mother how you were feeling?
8. Have you been afraid to question your mother's feelings?
9. Have you been afraid to have your own feelings if you knew your mother might not find them acceptable?
10. Have you felt uncomfortable having feelings you knew your mother would not like?

If you answered Yes to six or more questions, you can be sure that your mother has controlled your feelings. If you answered four or more questions with a Yes or Sometimes, you can be reasonably sure that she controlled your feelings.

4

The Survivor's Loyalty
to the Mother

Almost none of my clients' siblings were able or willing to stand up to the mother figure. Despite the fact that Enid's mother spent all the insurance money Enid (see pp. 27—28) received from her husband's death (Enid had given it to her mother for safekeeping at her mother's insistence), or that Norice's mother (see p. 8) spent all of her income on herself and demanded that her children pay her living expenses and buy her gifts, and despite these mothers' unwillingness to give up the abusers, all their children remained loyal except for the victims—and many of them remained loyal until therapy made such loyalty impossible. An extreme example of this type of loyalty is provided in the book *Memory Slips*, by concert pianist Linda Cutting. In it, Cutting tells how both of her brothers committed suicide rather than speak out against their mother.

ABIGAIL

Abigail's mother provides a striking example of this loyalty-inspiring characteristic. She not only allowed her second and third husbands to molest Abigail, but also her third husband's oldest son to molest Abigail—all the while enduring battering from both husbands that caused Abigail to hide in the closet with her sister, clutching a bigger-than-life-size teddy bear.

Although Abigail was finally, at age 36, able to face her "red hot" anger at her mother and stop displacing it onto her husband, children, and everyone else in her life, her sister (who presumably was not the target of abuse) never felt any emotion but admiration for their mother—even after their mother seduced her fiancé and had an affair with him lasting several years.

When Abigail first came for therapy, she had lost almost everything that mattered to her: a husband of 16 years, her nine-year-old son, and the house they had owned. The reason for these losses was Abigail's anger. She bullied, nagged, yelled, accused, and in other ways made life so miserable for her husband and three children that her husband threatened to leave. When he finally did, taking their nine-year-old son with him, Abigail realized she needed help.

Upon realizing in therapy that her mother was the real target of her anger, Abigail was able to express that anger in therapy and stop harassing her family. Her husband moved back in with her, and the family was reunited. Life was now better for all of them, and Abigail was happier than she had been in her entire life.

Then Abigail's mother began visiting her and her family every Sunday. Abigail began canceling therapy visits. During the few sessions she did attend, she said her mother had told her that she did not need therapy, that therapy was for whiners and self-pitiers, adding that Abigail did not "need to be telling family secrets to strangers." Abigail's sister and other members of her family called her frequently, accusing her of being disloyal to them by having therapy.

One part of Abigail knew these family members were wrong. But another part could not be disloyal to her mother. She tried continuing therapy, but the guilt and feelings of disloyalty were too much for her. After failing to show up for, or calling to cancel, three appointments, she stopped calling, and the agency closed her case. Every now and then Abigail calls, asks me how I am, and makes an appointment. "This time I'll keep it," she swears. But both she and I know she won't. She must remain loyal to her mother instead of to herself.

DEBORAH

Deborah's mother is an especially good example of the mother who inspires loyalty among all siblings—not by being strong, but by being weak. This woman's power lies in her ability to inspire worry and protectiveness in her seven children, both now and during all the years when the children were enduring incest from their father, his friends, and from their oldest brother, who is now a class one sex offender. All of these children except Deborah still believe their mother will succumb to bulimia, anorexia, self-mutilation, alcoholism, drug addiction, and various mental illnesses if they make any demands on her at all.

A lovely, articulate woman in her early twenties, Deborah worries constantly about her four brothers and two sisters, all of whom were subjected to abuse from their pedophile father. But she worries most about her mother, who believes herself to be the most victimized family member of all. At one point, Deborah recalls, her mother went to bed and "just didn't get up. Our dad was on disability and spent his days watching TV and molesting the younger kids. The state would bring us food boxes."

Did Deborah's mother care? "Oh, yes, I know she did. But she was so ill," Deborah said. "We were so worried about her all the time."

The care of the children fell to Deborah from the earliest time she can remember. From the age of six, she was seeing to the feeding, diapering, and bathing ("if the water hadn't been shut off!") of younger children while her mother languished in bed, providing instruction. "My main goal was to keep the little ones away from my dad," Deborah recalls. "If he took one of them away in his bedroom and shut the door, I knew..." Here, she shook her head, an expression of utter revulsion on her face.

And Deborah lived in fear of the "welfare people." "I always knew that if the welfare people knew what was going on in our house, they might take us kids away and put us in foster homes. That would have killed my mother—and me."

Finally, at age 16, Deborah had a complete breakdown, was hospitalized, and then spent six months recovering in a transition home. During that time, Deborah was silent about what was going on back home, again for fear of causing her mother to lose her "babies."

When sent home, she found that her mother was still lying in bed all day, with wet compresses on her head and the shades drawn. "She looked so pretty like that," Deborah recalls today with a smile. "Like a lovely illustration. She always wore these pretty old-fashioned nightgowns with puffy sleeves and lace at the neck."

About a year after her return, her father's abuse had escalated so badly that Deborah called Child Protective Services. The four children were removed from the house and placed in group homes. Her father, blaming Deborah, left home and married a former cheerleader who believed his assertions that Deborah had made up the abuse stories. Deborah's mother continued life as an invalid, now with anorexia, alcoholism (she drank wine all day), abuse of marijuana when her new drug-dealer boyfriend brought it over to her, and Vicodin, prescribed by doctors for her various pains.

Deborah came for therapy when her brother was caught molesting neighborhood children. Somehow, she felt, his condition was her fault. "If I'd just taken better care of him," she said, weeping. "My mother depended on me to make sure the kids were all right, and I let her down."

Today, Deborah lives on her own, trying to be self-sufficient. Her mother, currently trying to overcome her substance abuse problems, and the children live with stable grandparents, while the sex offender brother is on parole and lives with a friend.

Deborah suffers a loneliness she says she has always feared and now cannot bear. She's soothed it by visiting her mother, ignoring the usually inebriated boyfriend (who Deborah dislikes), and making sure her mother is all right. When her mother has a crisis, such as a fight with the still-violent sex offender brother on his visits, she calls Deborah. No matter the time of day or night, Deborah rushes over and takes her mother to the hospital. "I have to do it," she said when I suggested these frequent rescue missions might be interfering with her creating a life of her own. "My brothers and sisters expect me to do this and I want to do it. My mother means everything to me!"

But, Deborah's therapy has allowed her to see that no one in her family has ever taken care of her and she must now do so herself. Gradually, she is beginning to have a separate life. An artistic, sensitive person, she was thrilled when she got a job at an art gallery and is now happy with her artist boyfriend. She was relieved when her mother's boyfriend moved out, and even more relieved when a brother (not the sex offender) moved in. "Now, Mom has someone to take care of her who's real family." It took all Deborah's strength to say "No" when her mother wanted to move in with her. All of her family members called her constantly, accusing her of being disloyal to her mom. But

Deborah held her ground. "Mom needs constant care and I think it's someone else's turn to provide it. I have to work."

The fact that Deborah is enjoying her new life seems to enrage her family. They act out when they visit her at the gallery, getting in fights with her, and loudly disparaging the paintings. They "mess up my apartment, and never clean up after themselves," Deborah says. But she's learning it's all right to be loyal to herself, even if it means being perceived as disloyal to her family.

Her father and his new wife have adopted four-year-old twin boys. The wife works while the father stays home with the boys. Deborah worries about this arrangement, but feels there is nothing she can do. Her father still considers her a troublemaker and refuses to let her visit. His new wife told Deborah in a phone call that she wanted her to visit, and hoped that someday Deborah's father would lighten up. Meanwhile, she tells Deborah with a sigh, "You know how he is!"

Deborah does know how he is. She has told Child Protective Services how he is. And she has begged CPS to check on the adopted boys to make sure that her father is not molesting them. But who knows if CPS followed through? Deborah's father won't tell her, and CPS won't say.

I'm not optimistic. CPS recently had its budget cut and is now unlikely to respond to any call unless there is actual violence in the home.

5

The Mother's Destruction of the Survivor's Self-Esteem

Almost all of my clients have self-esteem issues. They feel that they not only deserved to be sexually abused, but might have brought it on themselves. Their only worth to others, they have learned, is sexual. But the sexual use made of them in their early years compounds their sense of shame and worthlessness. This sense of worthlessness in turn makes them more vulnerable to their mothers' attacks on their self-esteem. The message from their mothers is clear: "If you would just act in a worthwhile way, I wouldn't have to make you feel so worthless." But—and here's the real Catch 22—the survivor fears deep down that she can't act in a worthwhile way. If she did, she would be refuting her mother's opinion of her– proving her mother wrong. And to believe that her mother is wrong about anything is to risk making her mother furious enough to destroy her or, even worse, leave her and never come back. Zora's mother is a perfect example of this.

ZORA

Zora's parents grew up in aristocratic families in a South American country. Upon emigrating to the United States, Zora's father became a university professor and her mother a prominent faculty wife. Zora and her brother were beautiful, precocious children who were meticulously groomed at all times. Zora was a great source of pride to her family, not just for her beauty but also for her caring and sweet qualities. "I loved everybody," Zora says with a sad little smile.

Twice a year, Zora's mother took her to visit relatives in South America. On these visits, two of her aunts sexually abused Zora. At age four, Zora decided to disobey her aunts (who had told her never to tell) and confide in her mother about these incidents, saying she didn't like it when one aunt tied her up and the other did "nasty" things to her. Her mother told her that she was bad, "very, very bad," for saying such things about her saintly aunts, and was no longer a good, smart, pretty girl.

From that time on, Zora struggled to regain her status as the good, beloved child. But her mother remained cold and distant, accusing Zora of having evil intentions, refusing to hug her or provide any kind of loving affection. "It was like she had to show me how bad I really was because I was too dumb to know it!" Zora recalls.

When a female babysitter seduced Zora when Zora was seven, this seduction provided Zora with the kind of mothering she missed very much. Then she began to develop a subtly seductive persona with all women she liked and admired—a persona part caring and part temptress, a persona pursuing the validation she needed.

Zora's mother continued to denigrate and devalue her, telling her that she was lazy, worthless and incompetent. Every failure to excel in school and at chores at home led to a "See? You can't do anything right!" from her mother—and, eventually, from what Zora calls her "little voice inside," as well.

When Zora was 10, her father left her mother for another woman who had several bright, talented children. When Zora visited, she felt left out and inferior. When Zora was with her mother, she felt like "a terrible being, whose life should never have happened." Her mother's verbal abuse escalated after the divorce, now concentrating on Zora's unfolding beauty. "You look like a slut!" her mother would scream when Zora dressed up to go out with friends to the mall. "All you care about is yourself! You should be helping me, not out prowling like a whore!"

The attacks on Zora's self-esteem continued in many ways. When her mother was not making Zora feel worthless, she was making Zora feel guilty. "All you care about is leaving me," the mother would moan at least once a day. "That's all you want, after all I've done for you. Just to go off, move out, leaving me here alone!"

Zora began feeling hopeless; she was sure that she was not competent enough to live away from home, but that if she ever were, she couldn't leave because she would be abandoning her mother. Ever the good daughter, Zora found herself needing to live up (in reality, live down) to her mother's assessment of her competence, so she suffered severe anxiety whenever she did anything well or received any kind of award. Meanwhile, she continued to seek the affection she needed from boys and girls alike, becoming seductive when she felt needy. This behavior led to rejection from many girls she wanted to befriend. Those who accepted her offer of sexual conduct either used her for sex and then rejected her or became possessive, demanding more than she wanted to give.

When Zora was in her early teens, her mother began initiating conversations that were caring, that showed interest in Zora's life and activities. Zora would always get hooked into these conversations, thinking every time that she could confide her feelings to her mother and her mother would understand and love her. But, after getting Zora to confide her thoughts and feelings, Zora's mother would say things like, "Ugh! That's disgusting. You should have known better." "What were you thinking?" and "You'll never learn how to live your life."

By the time Zora was 18, she had no self-esteem at all. She thought she was stupid, "crazy," ugly, and fat; and she was desperate to escape her mother. In her three attempts to leave home, she was unable to support herself and ended up back with her mother, feeling worse than ever. When she attempted to hold a job, her mother would tell her the job was too menial and she should quit. Then when she did quit, her mother would tell her that she couldn't hold a job. In her attempts to have a social life, her mother told her that her friends were not good enough for her or were indecent or were otherwise unsuitable, and then, when Zora stopped seeing her friends, her mother told her that no one liked her because she was "such a mess" and that it was "no wonder you have no friends." When Zora asked her mother to help her buy a car so she could find a job, her mother said Zora wasn't stable enough mentally to drive. When Zora asked her mother for rides to interviews (there is no bus service in the area where her mother lives), her mother said she didn't have time and that Zora should be more self-sufficient: "Beg, beg, beg, that's all you do."

At age 16, Zora had a temper tantrum that triggered her mother to call 911 and put Zora in a mental hospital. As part of her treatment, the hospital gave Zora strong anti-psychotic medications that made her unable to stay awake in the daytime and unable to sleep at night. But still, Zora considered the hospital a positive experience. "It was being away from my home and my mother." Unafraid to go to the hospital from then on, Zora allowed herself to have two more temper tantrums, "so I could go to that hospital." Finally, the psychiatrist at the hospital realized that Zora had PTSD symptoms from childhood abuse and referred her to our agency.

"I know I'm stupid," Zora told me at her first session. She was also unconsciously seductive, as sexual abuse survivors tend to be—especially those women who have been abused by other women. She was also so beautiful, with her curvaceous figure, radiant complexion, and huge eyes, that everyone in the waiting room and front office stared at her in disbelief. It was quite amazing to hear her say that she knew she was ugly and fat, because nothing could be further from the truth.

But, thanks to her mother, Zora believes that she is ugly, fat, and stupid.

Zora's mother seems to have had two, and possibly three, reactions after hearing that Zora was sexually abused by relatives whose approval the mother valued. One was that Zora deserved the abuse because she was "bad." The other was anger at the relatives who abused Zora—anger she took out on Zora. The third possible reaction was sexual desire for Zora after Zora's mother divorced Zora's father.

Zora has internalized her mother's blame-the-victim mentality. She is ready to blame herself for everything that has happened to her, and believes she is bad in all the ways her mother says she is. Therapy is beginning to replace that inner belief with understanding that her mother is not right about her and that if she can get away from her mother and support herself, she will have a life. But it isn't easy for her to make these changes with her mother wearing her down at home. As of this writing, Zora's mother is telling her that therapy is not helping her, and that even though she may like her therapist she needs another one because she is making no real progress that her mother can see.

NILA

Nila's life shows how poor self-esteem induced by a mother does not clear up on its own, but escalates with time.

Nila is a sweet, gentle woman in her early sixties. When she was a child, Nila's mother told her that she was stupid, unappealing, and wasn't able to do anything right. Nila had six brothers and sisters who felt the same way about her. Never married to the fathers of her children, Nila's mother had a boyfriend who started abusing Nila when she was six. Her mother would send Nila to visit the boyfriend at his home in another state for "weeks at a time." During these visits, this man treated Nila like a sex toy, abusing her in any way and at any time he wanted. When Nila told her mother what happened, her mother accused her of being a bad girl who liked to get nice people in trouble. When Nila begged her mother not to send her to the boyfriend's house for visits, her mother told her to stop whining and to be sure to be a "good girl" for this man while she was visiting him. The abuse stopped (why, Nila never knew) only when the boyfriend married Nila's mother and moved into her home.

But Nila's sexual abuse was not over. At the age of nine, her mother sent her to visit an aunt and uncle, and the uncle sexually abused her every time the aunt was out on an errand. Nila's mother was furious at her for reporting this abuse, saying she "would never learn" to stop making things up about people who were "a lot nicer than you'll ever be. Your aunt and uncle were so nice to you while you were there—how you could say such terrible things about them just shows the kind of person you are."

Nila's mother continued to attack Nila's self-esteem, calling her "every name in the book that means stupid and dumb and embarrassing to her and not nice to be with." At 15, Nila married a man who was 29, "just to get out of the house." She had three sons in four years and endured verbal abuse during her ten-year marriage. She left her husband after finding out he was sexually abusing her eldest son. "I not only believed my son when he told me he was being abused, I sure did something about it," Nila said. "I packed us up and moved back in with my mother because there was no place else to go and I had my husband prosecuted and put in jail. It turned out he was wanted for other sexual abuse incidents and now he's got ten more years to go." Nila also put her son in therapy and found a counselor for herself.

Nila was beginning to respect herself for her ability to do something about her son's abuse. But moving back in with her mother was disastrous to her burgeoning self-esteem. Her mother yelled at her for having married a child abuser in the first place, for not being quiet about the abuse so she could have kept her husband, and for getting her and her kids' "meal ticket" put in jail so that now her mother had to take care of her.

Nila was soon out of the house again, married to another man who put her down, called her stupid, and criticized her housekeeping and everything else she did, but "at least didn't molest my kids." When she had the chance to leave this man for another man who "seemed really nice," Nila did so, only to find he turned "mean to me," too. When she left this man and got a job and apartment, one of her mother's brothers visited her one night. "I thought this uncle wanted to see my place and see how I was doing. But when the boys were asleep, he took out a knife and said if I did anything to wake up the boys, I would be killed and so would they. He raped me several times, then fell asleep. When I called my mother to come over and get him out of there, she said he was my problem, that he would never hurt anybody, and I must have wanted the sex." Nila wept bitterly as she recounted this story.

Now Nila's current partner, a man her age who has been divorced by his wife, is apparently living with Nila rent free in a home paid for by her meager social security checks. She has worked off and on for the past 30 years and has endured many abusive relationships with men. Her sons are now grown and married and not particularly willing to have her be a part of their lives. Her bad relationships and abusive partners have alienated her from her children almost entirely.

The worst part of Nila's life is that she misses her mother and can't figure out why. "I call her all the time, but she just calls me stupid and says I have nothing to show for myself and to stop calling her. But I can't stop and," here Nila always dissolves into tears, "I don't know why." The reason why is simple. Nila can't give up hope that her mother will tell her that she's fine and will give her the approval she has craved since childhood.

This addiction to the parent—either to the mother and/or to the abuser—is very common in survivors who have lost all self-esteem. They see their enabling mother, the source of their poor self-esteem, as the only person who has the power to raise their self-esteem—the only one who can tell them they are now all right, are doing well, are lovable, are worthy of respect, and of being treated well. The betraying mother's few tender moments with the survivor (there are always some of these moments to hold on to) are seen as proof that the mother did believe in the survivor's goodness and worth and talent and did enjoy her. The need for more of these moments never, apparently, dies. The survivor finds it almost impossible to believe that she needs to give up, because these moments are never going to happen again. So, the survivor keeps trying to contact the mother, hoping, praying, and always believing that this time things will be different—this time the mother will say the admiring, respectful, delightful things the survivor desperately longs to hear. This need to reach out to the enabling mother often becomes an impulse the survivor cannot control.

Ironically, Nila's response to her oldest son's sexual abuse was probably instrumental in his being able to have a happy, successful life with a good career in banking, and a happy marriage with a beautiful woman who, like this son, does not want to have children. Unfortunately, her son's wife finds Nila needy and "sad—she says I'm too sad!" and does not want Nila visiting except at Christmas and Thanksgiving every other year. And this woman does not want Nila associating with her family, with whom she and Nila's son spend a great deal of time.

Nila goes on feeling that she is a failure, unappealing, bad at cleaning, cooking, and other domestic chores, and too stupid to have a career. In therapy, she is seeing how her mother controlled her self-esteem. She is also getting in touch with how angry she is at her mother and has vented a lot of rage. These are her first steps toward being able to feel good about herself.

Did your mother control your self-esteem?

Answer every question Yes, No, or Sometimes.

1. Did your mother ever call you "stupid" or some other name that demeaned your intelligence?
2. Did your mother ever call you "ugly," "fat," or some other name that demeaned your appearance?
3. Did your mother ever tell you that you weren't any good at doing something?
4. Did your mother ever tell you that you were incapable of doing something, such as driving a car or babysitting?
5. Did your mother ever tell you that you were untalented at something?
6. Did your mother ever make you feel that you were bad and could not possibly do anything to make yourself better?
7. Did your mother ever tell you that you should do something about your hair, your weight, and/or your skin?
8. Did your mother ever indicate disgust at the way you looked?
9. Did your mother tell you that you were bad somehow for being tired, depressed, and/or disappointed about something?

Just one Yes answer could mean that your mother controlled your self-esteem. Two Yes answers mean that she wanted to control your self-esteem. Three or more Yes answers mean she probably did control your self-esteem.

6

The Mother's Emotional Alienation of the Survivor

The mothers described in this book not only have the ability to make their abused children feel left out of the family, these mothers actually engineer the situations and family dynamics by which the victims are excluded. And, it seems, these mothers enjoy knowing the survivors are left out.

GUDRUN

Gudrun, a 35-year-old survivor of abuse from her father and his brothers from the age of four to eight, and from her two adopted brothers from the age of 13 to 15, is happily married to a college professor and has four well-adjusted children. Gudrun was a college professor of education until about five years ago, when she was triggered by a newspaper story about a young girl who killed herself at the age of 13 because she could not escape her father's sexual abuse.

Suddenly, Gudrun was having flashbacks, anger attacks, and crying spells that left her unable to work or be intimate with her husband. Her primary caregiver referred her to our agency when she described the flashbacks, and he realized that she was reliving childhood sexual abuse. Gudrun had never received any therapy for her abuse and had not had any PTSD symptoms until she was triggered—a common sequence for survivors who experienced few or no symptoms at the time the abuse was ongoing and/or stopped. The onset of symptoms years later is especially disturbing for a survivor because she has long believed the abuse was behind her and that she need not think about it ever again.

The reason why Gudrun never sought therapy for her abuse, until she was 35, was that her mother told her that the abuse never happened, and that if it did, Gudrun was responsible for it—her brothers were good boys and would never do such a thing if not teased and taunted by the seductive little Gudrun. "That is so untrue," Gudrun told me, sobbing. "I was about the most unseductive little girl you could imagine, and such a goody two shoes. Why she even thought I would do that is beyond me." Her mother's accusation was amazing to me, too, because Gudrun's mother is a prominent psychiatrist who should have learned about the effects of childhood sexual abuse in her medical school training, or should have found out about those effects if they weren't covered in her medical school courses. But she not only continued to blame Gudrun for causing the abuse—if Gudrun were not making it up—she all but excommunicated Gudrun from the family and devoted her attention not just to Gudrun's brothers, but to their girlfriends as well. "It was as if the girlfriends were the daughters she wanted," Gudrun recalls. "My mother was always giving them gifts, taking them on trips, referring them for medical care, and having them over for dinner." Gudrun, meanwhile, was never taken on family trips—"I was told I couldn't behave myself properly and no one wanted me around"—or given any medical care. Gudrun remembers being covered with an oozing, bright skin rash at the age of five that her mother ignored until her school principal said she could not return to school until the rash was treated, and also having toothaches that her mother ignored all through her childhood and adolescence until the aching teeth had to be extracted. As a result, she says, "I have only my front teeth left."

Family photos from Gudrun's childhood show her always far off to the side, not smiling, and looking as though she knows she does not fit in. Her brothers and parents are always in the center, smiling happily, looking like a close family.

When Gudrun was pregnant with her first child, her mother never called to see how she was and didn't come to the hospital for the birth. And—most amazingly for a grandmother—never came to see the baby until Gudrun begged her to, and then she stayed only a few minutes, never holding the baby at all. Yet Gudrun's mother was extremely attentive during the pregnancies, births, breastfeedings, and other baby activities of her son's wives. "And," Gudrun said in therapy, "I was her only daughter—and her real child. It's just beyond me."

It would have been beyond me, too, had I not "known" this kind of mother by the time I was counseling Gudrun. The fact that this was "unbelievable" behavior is important. The truth is that it was so unbelievable that nobody could see it was happening—not even Gudrun. "At the time, I just thought I was included in the family, that it was my fault that I felt left out or neglected or pushed out of the way by my mother. I felt it was my fault for feeling bad about it, and I felt like if it was happening, then I was bringing it on myself by the way I was, by some quality in me that was just so unappealing it was no wonder my mother didn't want me with the boys and their girlfriends and wives. I kept hoping things would change."

And Gudrun kept wanting, and being addicted to, her mother's attention. At the time she came in for therapy, she was still calling her mother every week, still being treated with coldness and indifference, still going over and over those few comments from her mother that might indicate a maternal feeling, a real bond Gudrun could count on. And Gudrun was unable to stop making these calls even though she knew "I would be depressed, seriously depressed, the rest of the day and sometimes the whole week after I called her, until it got near time when I thought I could call her again. Then I'd get hopeful again and that would replace the depression—till, of course, I made the next call and got depressed all over again."

When Gudrun told her mother about this cycle in a desperate attempt to change her mother's response, her mother told her, "You're 35 years old, for God's sake. You should be over this sort of neediness by now!"

The accusation of being needy was what Gudrun dreaded most. "If I did anything to be included in the family, like ask to go on a trip or go somewhere with mom and one of the boys' girlfriends, that was it. That was enough to make her say, 'Oh, Gudrun, please, you are *so* needy! You should be ashamed.'" And of course Gudrun would be.

Gudrun said she almost welcomed the sexual abuse from her brothers in her teenage years, despite dreading and fearing what they would do to her every time they attacked her. "At least it was attention. I always hoped it might make them like me more, but it never did."

In therapy, Gudrun began to realize that her brothers' abuse of her kept them from going too far sexually with the sainted girlfriends so special to their mom.

Where was Gudrun's father all this time? "He was traveling the country going to conferences and seminars. He'd come home just long enough to get fresh clothes and go somewhere with the boys and mom and their girlfriends. I never knew who he was, really. There was never any time." He died at age 50 from a brain aneurysm.

Gudrun is still releasing repressed anger at her mother in therapy—layers and layers of it that sometimes result in 50 minutes of crying and recalling how she felt when, for instance, she saw the family come home after a weeklong camping trip "all tanned and happy" after they had left her at home with her aunt, who was as distant as her mother, or a sitter. Or watching while her mother wrapped "mountains" of baby gifts for her brother's wife's first baby, "looking just so sweet and loving and grandmotherly." The only thing her mother has said to her in the time Gudrun has been in therapy is that Gudrun should stop therapy at once, because dwelling on negative things will "only make [her] feel worse."

When Gudrun is ready, she might be able to see that she finally has something her family doesn't have—therapy that she says is working for her and helping her feel good about herself for the first time in her life. That realization might be a satisfaction Gudrun allows herself to enjoy.

Gudrun's husband and children love her dearly. This love is somewhat surprising, because I know that Gudrun has always put her mother before them. That this love exists attests to the fact that in spite of everything she has suffered, and is still suffering, Gudrun has been a wonderful wife and mother—even though her mother would never let her be proud of that or anything else.

*   *   *

Other clients must behave in certain ways in the family or they become emotional outcasts. Larry, for instance, if he wanted to be included in family events, had to act as though his father were just obeying a normal impulse in molesting Larry's siblings. Norice was expected to babysit, loan money, and in other ways assist her mother and other siblings if she wanted to be invited to reunions and kept in the family gossip loop.

All of the survivors discussed here are emotionally alienated from their mothers. But as life goes on, and the incest either continues or stops, the mother's alienation of its victim becomes entrenched. The sacrificing of the victim child for the other children becomes a way of life for the whole family. If the victim child tells a sibling of the abuse, the response is often, "Oh, she always makes bad stuff up. That's why we never pay attention to her." The rest of the family has become as emotionally alienated from the survivor as the mother. Yes, one or two might at times feel sorry for excluding the victim, but the feeling seldom lasts. It's just too easy to maintain the status quo because, as the others in the family know, it is exactly what the mother really wants.

The betraying mother also alienates the victim by making herself unavailable when needed. Every time my clients ask their mothers for any kind of help, their mothers refuse. Zora once called her mother to come pick her up from my office when her session was over, as her mother had told her to do, only to have her mother tell her that she was too busy to come for her, so she should call a friend. Two-and-a-half hours later, Zora was still in the office lobby, on the phone, trying to find a ride. When I asked Zora why her mother had changed her mind, Zora told me with a very defeated look, "She always does this. I'm not surprised." Another example is Nila's mother refusing to take her drunken brother from Nila's house after he raped Nila.

These and many other incidents perpetrated by the betraying mothers described in this book show how they engineered the emotional alienation of the survivors in ways that were not only painful, but unsupportive and unkind as well.

Did your mother alienate you from other family members?

Answer every question Yes, No, or Sometimes.

1. Did you ever feel like you were on the outside of your family looking in?
2. Did you ever want to be suddenly rich or beautiful or courted by a famous person so your family would respect you?
3. Did you ever feel great jealousy of a sibling or cousin?
4. Did you ever discover that your mother had planned family events in which you were not included?
5. Did you ever find out that your mother had given your siblings, cousins, or other family members something you did not know about?
6. Did you ever feel that your mother wished that you did not participate in family activities?
7. Did you ever feel that your mother was trying to eliminate your communication with other family members?
8. Did you ever feel that your family's interactions were a constant party you weren't really invited to?
9. Did your mother ever tell you that you were not nice, polite, or attractive enough to socialize with other family members?
10. Did you long for inclusion in your family and resent your exclusion?

Three or more Yes or Sometimes answers indicate that your mother alienated you from her and from other family members.

7

The Mother's Scapegoating
of the Survivor

It is clear from innumerable statements by my clients that their mothers dislike them.

KATYA

A redhead in her early twenties, Katya grew up in a kind of commune, with her own and three other families living in the same house. Her father's brother—Katya's uncle—was the father of one of the families; her father's cousins were the heads of the others. "It was like these guys just grew up being really close, stayed close while they were dating, and then decided to live together after they got married and had kids," Katya explained. "It was fine with their wives; everybody got along. We had this huge old Victorian house with many wings that was actually built to house extended families. We were always working on the house, improving it in some way. That was fun. I loved it. The kids all loved it. We had instant playmates, all the time."

It was, Katya added, "a great way to raise families. There was always some adult to talk to if your own parents weren't available."

But when Katya was six, one of the men began to abuse her. "He would wake me up at night and take me to the attic." Katya could not say "No," because she was afraid to and also because this attention made her feel special. "He was so sweet to me," Katya recalled. "He said I was beautiful and that I gave him such pleasure. And he gave me pleasure, too." Katya felt terribly guilty about that pleasure, but also became addicted to it.

"It was like I had a double life for almost three years," Katya recalls. "A child mistress at night and a child by day, playing with this man's kids and spending a lot of time with his wife, whom I adored. I was actually closer to her than to my own mom." Katya's mom had less time for Katya than her abuser's wife, because Katya's mother was a sort of executive director of the sprawling household. She collected the mortgage and utilities monies, paid the bills, supervised maintenance, did the food shopping, oversaw the kitchen duties schedule, and chaired the weekly house meetings. "She was very competent at all that stuff," Katya said. "I was so proud of her— it was like my mom was boss of everybody in the house, but in a nice way. I went to Lili [her abuser's wife] for my owwies and kid problems."

Then, when she was almost nine, Katya suddenly couldn't stand her abuse anymore. "I don't know what came over me," she said, "but I had to tell somebody about it—unfortunately, I told Lili. I just blurted it out, probably because I told her everything anyway. I didn't stop to think that it was her husband doing the abusing."

Amazingly, Lili had her husband arrested for child abuse and put in jail within 24 hours. She was open and honest with everybody about why she did so, and how she meant to prosecute to the full extent of the law and file for divorce. Everyone in the house admired Lili's courage and chipped in to pay her and her children's expenses until she could find a job. And, Katya recalls, "everyone was very nice to me—except my mom."

Katya's mother stopped talking to her, became cold, and blamed her for bringing "trouble" on the house. "Now the police will be watching this place," Katya's mother yelled at her daughter. "The child protection people will be watching this place. Now this place has a bad reputation, all because of you." All Katya had to do, her mother said with great disdain, was tell her, her own mother, what was happening and her mother would have seen to it that the abuse stopped and the abuser never bothered her again. "He's not a bad man, for God's sake," her mother added in what Katya recalls as a "hissing" voice. "He's just got a little problem with little girls. A lot of men have that. It's nothing to get so heated up about. Now you've ruined his entire life! And his kids' lives, and maybe a lot of other people's lives as well."

For the next several years, Katya's mother intensely disliked her. Her mother was always blaming her for something or other at the house meetings, which she forced Katya to attend. The other people living in the house soon got the idea that being disdainful of Katya was a way to "get in good" with her mother. And, anyway, it was good to have a scapegoat they could blame for all of the children's bad behaviors. The children would taunt Katya in ways that made her act out at them (such as calling her "slut," "c....sucker," and other abusive names) and then tell on her for getting mad at them. Katya's mother always dismissed her explanations.

Lili remained kind to her, but could not protect her from the others. And Katya was filled with guilt for having "done all those things with Lili's husband that he should have been doing with Lili."

Katya moved out of the house at 16 to become a live-in nanny. At 17, she became a student in a local college, and will graduate next year with a BA in physical education, which she hopes to teach.

Unfortunately, Katya is still suffering from the effects of her childhood sexual abuse and her mother's treatment. She has had a string of affairs with boys who were involved in relationships with other girls and cheated with Katya in secret. Although she finally did get one of these boys to leave his girlfriend for her, the relationship went downhill after they became a couple. He treated Katya so abusively emotionally, calling her names and blaming her for his problems, that she decided he was better for her when he was with his girlfriend.

Katya is also addicted to being with her mother, who has divorced Katya's father, moved out of the house, and in with a new man who may become Katya's stepfather. Katya is always wanting to visit her mother and then wanting to leave after about an hour because of her mother's blame, accusations, and criticism. "She tries to like me at first on these visits, but can't bring it off," Katya says sadly. "So she just putters around, dusting or something, not really paying attention to me anymore, while I just sit there, trying to think of something to say. It's awful."

But Katya can't give up the hope that on the next visit her mom will like her. "What's wrong with me? I can't stop thinking she'll change! Yet I know she won't."

There is, of course, nothing wrong with Katya for thinking her mother will change. Every child needs her mother, goes on needing her mother, and goes on thinking her mother will some day be nice to her.

Katya is now working through her layers of guilt– guilt for succumbing to the abuse (she is just now realizing that she had no choice, that abusers groom children in ways that render them powerless), guilt for not telling her mom, guilt for letting the abuse go on for so long, guilt for telling Lili, guilt for making everyone in the house vulnerable to police inspection, and guilt for making her mom so mad at her. She also feels very guilty—although she has trouble admitting it—for missing her abuser's attentions for several years after the abuse stopped. "I still fantasize about him now," she admits. "That is just so awful of me. But at least he liked me! I don't think anyone likes me now—but you."

Of course it's not "awful" to miss the abuse. Like many children, Katya found her abuse physically and emotionally pleasurable while it was ongoing. She responded in normal sexual ways, as even very young children can do.

But, thanks to her mother, Katya is unable to forgive herself. She's also unable to stop acting out her abuse by choosing men who are either with someone else or, if she gets them all to herself, mistreat her in ways she may secretly think she deserves. Her mother's dislike and scapegoating of her confirms Katya's belief that she will never deserve happiness and true love, not after all the bad things she's done.

A question I posed to Katya might help her deal with her guilt. How, I asked, was her abuser able to get away with the abuse for so long without getting caught? It seems impossible that no one else in the house knew what was going on. Two or three nights a week the abuser would wake Katya in the room she shared with two other children, go hand in hand with her through the house and up the stairs to the attic. Surely someone had to notice. In all probability, several people were aware of this and reported it to Katya's mom, the "boss" of the house. It's also probable that Katya's mom told them it was nothing or made some excuse and said not to mention it again. I think it quite likely that Katya's mother betrayed Katya by enabling her abuser. I could be wrong—but, unfortunately, I doubt that I am.

A therapist's greatest challenge in helping abuse survivors is dealing with their internalization of their mothers' words, even after they leave their mothers and go off on their own. They keep hearing a blaming voice. Sometimes the voice is someone else's, sometimes the voice is the client's own voice. In either case, the clients can't help but think that the voice is right: they are worthless, guilty, bad. With enough therapy, survivors begin to realize that the voice is wrong, and they stop paying attention to it. The clients are much happier when they are able to silence this voice, and so am I.

Did your mother dislike you and/or make you a scapegoat?

Answer every question Yes, No, or Maybe

1. Did your mother ever blame anything on you?
2. Did your mother ever blame you for bad luck in the family?
3. Did your mother express dislike of you in any way?
4. Did your mother ever say she wanted to love or like you, but couldn't?
5. Did your mother ever tell anyone else in your family she didn't like you?
6. Did your mother ever blame you for your disappointments in life?
7. Did your mother ever say she didn't know why your friends liked you?
8. Did your mother ever say you were not good enough for your significant other, your friends, your siblings, or anyone else?
9. Did your mother ever blame you for her problems in life?
10. Did you ever feel guilty about your mother's problems in life?

One or two Yes or Maybe answers mean that your mother might not have liked you and might have made you a scapegoat. Three or more Yes or Maybe answers mean that your mother disliked you and used you as a scapegoat.

8

The Resilience of the Enabling Mother

Resilience means the ability to go on with one's life in the face of bad luck, tragedy, or any kind of adversity. It also means the ability to do well for oneself no matter what the obstacles.

Many of my clients' mothers are resilient. Despite their children's sexual abuse at the hands of their partner or some other close relative(s), the mothers are able to go on with their own lives, to pursue successful careers, and to have positive relationships with other children and new partners. In other words, they are able to make their lives work not just well, but often very well.

Meanwhile, the survivors find their lives at a standstill. They remain emotionally devastated, in need of psychiatric medication, unable to tolerate relationships with anyone or, in many cases, even to live independently. Sometimes a survivor goes on to do well in the outside world by dint of sheer willpower and tenacity. In these cases, the abused child remains alive, still there inside the survivor's brain and body, able to watch the survivor move on with her life while being unable to move on with her. Sometimes that child becomes so separate from the survivor that it takes on its own personality and a life of its own, which can emerge into the survivor's "real" life at any time. If there is not another personality to deal with, the survivor must deal with the other issues we have already seen: guilt for her participation in the abuse (again, survivors always think there was something they could have done to make the abuser stop, even if they were only a toddler); guilt for the effect of the abuse on other family members; guilt for pleasure in the sexual aspects of the abuse; and guilt for anger at her mother, the person she wants to please more than anyone else in the world. Then there is guilt for not being able to have sex with her partner, if she has one, and guilt for her involuntary PTSD symptoms —crying spells, flashbacks, mysterious phobias, panic attacks, fear of being attacked in even well-lit, safe places—she thinks she should be over. The survivor feels especially guilty when her children witness these symptoms. And there is even worse guilt for the self-medication with liquor, drugs, and prescription pills many survivors resort to when things get too bad. "Weak, weak, I'm just so weak," is how one client puts it when she takes another Valium to get rid of unbearable feelings of guilt. "I feel so guilty for being so weak."

Many of the survivors' mothers spend energy and time on their own success, while ignoring the needs of their survivor children. Gudrun's mother has become the head of a psychiatric agency that gets many grants and makes millions from contracts with other agencies. Thanks to her business success, Zora's mother now presides over a huge home in a very expensive area. Larry's mother recovered from the horror of her husband's abuse of their children to become mistress of an academic empire that exists to support the family's degree-seeking and publication activities.

Norice's mother lives like a revered religious figure, collecting what amounts to weekly tithes from the 26 or so family members who live nearby. "You have to give her some of your money every month," Norice told me, "or she won't speak to you. Everybody (in the family) hates that, so they pay up. If she doesn't think it's enough, she lets you know." What does Norice's mom do in return for this largesse? "She sits all day and watches TV and lets people come visit. You'll find several people at her house just sitting and talking and watching the TV shows with her all day long." Sometimes Norice's mother goes on trips to resorts to rest her nerves. But, Norice said, beginning to cry, "she won't come visit me. I've begged her a million times and said I would pay her fare, but she won't do it. And I'm only three hours away." Norice's mother appears never to give, only to take—and no one in the family except Norice objects.

Did your mother show resilience when you were suffering?

Answer every question Yes, No, or M (for "Most of the time").

1. Did your mother ever tell you to "move on" or "get over it" when you were affected by a PTSD symptom?
2. Is your mother doing well now?
3. Does your mother normally refuse to talk about your abuse?
4. Is your mother taking care of her own needs on a regular basis?
5. Does your mother make you feel left out of her life?
6. Does your mother ever say that she was abused and look how well she is doing?
7. Does your mother make you feel that your needs are interfering with her life?
8. Does your mother seem like a success to people outside the family?
9. Do you consider your mother a person you can never hope to be like?
10. Does your mother make you feel that you do not share in her success?

Four or more Yes or M answers mean that your mother is resilient and is more concerned with her life than yours.

The Enabling Mother's Self-Image as a Good Parent

Almost all of the mothers described in these pages believe themselves to be excellent homemakers and child rearers; others also believe that they are exemplary parents. Colin's mother is a good example.

COLIN

Although Colin's uncles subjected him to sexual abuse on their annual hunting trips, it did not even slightly affect his mother's image of herself as a good wife and even better mother. Her home was run like a well-kept resort for her husband, his many relatives, and his business associates. A prominent peace officer in his state, Colin's father has a great deal of power and fame. He is now in high office and, according to Colin, "is looking to go a lot higher." Unfortunately, Colin doesn't know much about his father at this time because Colin left his family during his late teenage years.

Colin was his father's only child, born shortly after his father graduated from the police academy. Colin's mother was a stay-at-home wife with an interest in the domestic arts; Colin's earliest memories are of his mother's various crafts endeavors. "She made everything in the house: the drapes, the slipcovers for the furniture, the rugs even, out of rags. She was always cutting, sewing, and she just about lived in those big stores where they sell all the craft stuff."

Because his father was too busy at his job to spend much time with Colin, Colin was more his mom's son than his dad's. "I was kind of puny and got bullied by the other kids in the neighborhood. My dad would get disgusted because I wouldn't get in fights and my mom would just tell me to stay away from those kids and help her around the house."

But that life didn't please Colin very much. "I didn't like that girlie stuff. I lived for the times I could be with my dad. He was my hero, even if he didn't seem to like me much." Colin remembers being thrilled the few times his father played catch with him. "I'd be so excited I'd fumble the ball and not be able to catch the ball and he'd get disgusted with me and quit after about 10 minutes."

When Colin was six, his father decided to take him on his annual hunting trip to the woods. "Thrilled? That's not even the word for how happy I was," Colin said. "I just couldn't believe my dad wanted me to be with him for a whole ten days." When they got to the hunting lodge, Colin found several of his dad's friends and relatives already there, enjoying masculine camaraderie away from "the wives." Colin said he felt uneasy in all that male company, but tried desperately to fit in.

The next day, Colin's father went off alone to "get moose" while Colin stayed behind. By lunchtime, the men at the lodge "were drunk on beer and eating no food but chips and pretzels." Colin said he felt "really left out and ignored" by these men, until one of them called him over to his chair and said it was time to inspect his genitalia to see how it was growing. "He asked me if I wanted to drink a beer and of course I sad yes."

Within an hour, most of the men had fondled Colin and had given him oral sex lessons. "I hated it, I was scared and disgusted. But I didn't know how to get them to stop it. I couldn't say no, I was scared they'd get mad at me." After a few more beers, Colin was able to endure the abuse, but never lost his sense of fear and disgust.

When Colin's dad returned from his hunting trip that night, not a word was said about what had happened to Colin that day. Colin spent the next nine days hunting with his dad and the other men, but he found himself so ashamed that he couldn't enjoy being with his dad and couldn't look any of the other men in the eye. "It was like I brought that sex on myself, somehow. I felt like used goods."

"I told Dad about the sex abuse on the trip home," Colin said. "He just reached over and backhanded me so hard I got a nosebleed. He said not to make up those kind of stories and never mention it again."

When asked if his mother ever knew, Colin said she didn't want to know. "I tried to tell her. I said, 'Mom, they did bad things to me,' but she said something like she didn't want to know, that men did stuff when they were alone that women didn't like hearing about, and I was a man and I had to get used to it."

The rest of the year after he was abused at the hunting lodge, Colin repressed what had happened to him. He went back to longing—fruitlessly—for his father's attention. When his father said he was taking Colin on the annual hunting trip again the next year, Colin was glad. "All I knew was I would get to be with my dad again. I had completely got over the other part and I was sure it wouldn't happen again."

It did happen again. It was worse this time because more penetration was attempted and Colin, knowing what was coming, cried and begged them to stop from the beginning. "But that only made things worse. They called me sissy boy and said they could give me something to cry about [the penetration]." This time when he got home, Colin didn't "even bother trying to talk to [his] mom." He told an uncle who believed him, but said there was nothing he could do. From then on, that uncle invited Colin to visit him and his family every year during the times of the hunting trips. "I think my uncle said something to my dad and my dad decided it was better if I went somewhere else than on the hunting trip."

Since then, Colin has developed full-blown PTSD, which keeps him from sleeping, eating, being able to be with men without fear, and and makes him want to get "very drunk" every year at the time of the hunting trips. He no longer drinks or uses drugs, but he has been married three times and cannot keep a job. He was determined for years to get into the police academy, and tried ROTC, but was unable to be with the type of men in those organizations for very long—much as he wanted to believe he was like them.

Colin is receiving treatment for his PTSD, but his new wife is undermining it in many ways. A housekeeper *par excellence* like his mother, this woman insists he is fine, that his symptoms are all in his head, and that he find a way to make more money so he can get her a better house.

Colin's mother would find that she has a lot in common with her son's wife if she got to know her, but she has put Colin out of her life.

She is now known all over the state for her barbeques, open houses, campaign headquarters décor, and other homemaking talents. She is always available for interviews with feature reporters and is a great asset to her husband, who is now in political office and who also holds a prominent role in the private prison field.

BRIDGET AND NANCY

In the cases of Bridget and Nancy, both Irish girls subjected to incest by their brothers from their earliest years, their mothers had so many children that they saw them as "broods" to be fed, clothed, cleaned, educated and brought up Catholic. Both Bridget's and Nancy's mothers not only handled these childcare jobs in exemplary ways, but they kept a "fine house," as Bridget put it. Bridget remembers going visiting with her mom as a little girl, all dressed up in pretty dresses with her hair curled and "smiling, smiling, smiling," while suffering "secret dread" all the time. The dread, she learned after retrieving some early childhood memories in therapy, was caused by the constant threat of being raped at any time by one or more of her older male cousins.

Nancy's mother, a poet, was less perfectionistic than Bridget's mother, and more of a free spirit. "Her life was spent creating a home full of music, art, and creative expression. She was always having local artists and professors in for discussions and poetry readings. She would take in kids from city ghettos every summer so they could enjoy my mom and her home."

Meanwhile, this mother's four sons and many male cousins were brutalizing Nancy in various sexual ways. Nancy thinks her sisters might have been molested, too, but they won't say. One is always in rehab centers with alcohol problems, while the other is living in Ireland, now a mother of seven herself.

Did Bridget and Nancy tell their mothers about the incest in their beautifully kept homes? Both say they tried to, but got almost identical responses: "Just stay away from those boys and tell them to leave you alone." And then their mothers would say they had some chore to attend to or would change the subject completely. "It was like," Nancy recalls, "a part of my mother's brain just was not going to compute that information."

Both Bridget and Nancy adored their mothers when they were children and still love them to this day. In one sense they are angry that their mothers didn't try harder to find out what was going on. But both felt loved enough by their mothers to believe that their mothers' denial of their sexual assaults was not intentional and might have even been a necessary reaction considering how hard each one had to work in order to "keep up" their beautiful, welcoming homes and large families.

I am not so forgiving. I believe Bridget's and Nancy's mothers were good in many ways. But in order to be "good mothers" to their other kids, they were willing to sacrifice one child. Perhaps, as both Bridget and Nancy suspect, their mothers were themselves sexually abused by their numerous brothers in their childhoods and had to learn how to survive on their own. They might have felt that such treatment is a little girl's lot in life, and it's a little girl's job to deal with it. It's interesting that neither Bridget nor Nancy wants children of her own.

Most of the mothers in this book could actually be said to be good parents in many respects. They made sure their babies' physical needs were met and that they survived to become adults. They managed most of their children's childhoods in ways that allowed physical and intellectual growth. But a good mother, even to great numbers of children, would never sacrifice a child to ongoing sexual abuse.

Does your mother consider herself a good parent?

Write True or False after every statement.

1. My mother is very concerned about her reputation as a mother.
2. My mother blames her children for things that indicate she might not be a good parent.
3. My mother said she had no way of stopping my abuse.
4. My mother said the abuse had nothing to do with her.
5. My mother made sure her children looked nice at all times.
6. My mother cared more about how her children behaved than about how they felt.

7. My mother told me not to talk to anyone about my abuse.

8. My mother made me feel like an employee in her home, an employee who had better perform her duties correctly.

9. I feel like I don't have a mother, even though the rest of the world sees her as being terrific.

10. People tell me I'm lucky to have a mother like mine, and I think something's wrong with me for her not giving me the understanding I need, especially about my abuse.

Two or more True answers mean that your mother thinks of herself as a good parent and is not worried that you might disagree.

10

The Survivor's Relationship to the Perpetrator's New Wives/Girlfriends

Often, my clients' mothers divorced their abusing husbands—not because of the abuse, to my clients' knowledge, but for other reasons. What is astonishing is that women who knew that these now-single fathers had been accused of abuse married them anyway. "It's as though," one client said, "these new wives think of a man they love as a blank slate with all past sins wiped clean." Or they think of him as a flawed person whom they can make virtuous again. Mostly, I believe, it is a case of the new wife or girlfriend deciding (often deliberately) that if it is true that perpetrator sexually abused his own child, he was driven to it by a "bad," that is, seductive and possessive, child, and by his ex-wife's failure to meet his needs.

Typically, such new relationships have three outcomes.

One is that the survivor is forced by the new stepparent to be an outsider in her own family, often supplanted in favor and financial largesse by the new stepmother's biological children. This is what happened to Enid in some respects. (See pp. 35—36)

The second outcome is that the survivor bonds with the new stepmother and has to watch her become emotionally destroyed by the perpetrator. This seems to be happening to the "cheerleader" woman who married Deborah's father (see pp. 50—53): "The last time I saw Missy [her abuser dad's new wife] she looked so sad and defeated, she couldn't even hold her head up and her hair wasn't combed."

The third outcome is that the survivor tries desperately to insinuate herself into the stepmother's affections and lives in a state of yearning until she realizes she is never going to get what she wants. Nila experienced this fate. (See pp. 59—61)

This is also what happened to Claudia, a woman who is now 50 and starting over in life after several psychotic episodes.

CLAUDIA

Claudia's biological mother moved away after divorcing Claudia's father when Claudia was just a toddler, and made it clear she did not want any children in her life. Claudia then began trying to please a succession of girlfriends and live-in stepmothers, all the while enduring oral sex and fondling from her father. After her father remarried, Claudia tried very hard to please her new stepmother. But the jealousy she felt over this woman's place in her father's sex life became impossible to bear. In a rage one night at dinner, she disclosed her abuse by her father, screaming that she had "loved every minute of it." But the new wife replied coldly that the abuse was in the past, "before I knew this man."

From then on, the woman gave Claudia just enough hope to keep her dangling. "I thought she liked me. I cleaned the house, I did my stepmother's nails, and when I was a teenager, I did most of the care of her mom, who came to live with us. I thought of this woman as my grandma and did everything for her, and even got trained as a nurse's aide so I would be more qualified. It was hard, too, because that woman had Alzheimer's."

When Claudia's father suddenly left her stepmother for another woman, Claudia thought she would still "be this woman's daughter and her mom's granddaughter. But they up and moved back to Idaho, where they came from, and I never heard from them again. I wrote and wrote and called and called, but they never called back."

Claudia ran away and became a drug abuser and prostitute. But today Claudia is clean and sober, living in a shelter and trying to be a family of one.

Thanks to meds, three-times-a-week therapy, and the companionship of the other people in the shelter, Claudia is beginning to feel as though she belongs somewhere with someone. But she's still tempted to call her stepmother and ask if she can come out for a visit, a "real no-no," Claudia says, because she knows the stepmother is as finished with her as she is with Claudia's dad.

GERMAINE

Germaine's case illustrates the first outcome, being supplanted by the new stepmother (in this case, girlfriends) and the third, wishing for a relationship with the new girlfriends.

I was especially astonished by the case of Germaine, who was used by her single father as a mistress from the time she was 14 until she was 18, while he was also having affairs. "These women knew what he was doing with me," Germaine said. "That's because he loved bragging about what he was doing. And they didn't care! They'd be all bitchy to me when they came over or called him on the phone, like I was the competition they were going to get him away from. I couldn't believe it! And worst of all, I was so jealous, I wanted to claw their eyes out, too!" I also found it hard to believe—and worked with Germaine on her feelings of jealousy, which she came to see were perfectly normal.

Germaine was living with her father because her mother had left him and was remarried to a man who had no desire to have Germaine in his life. Her mother never visited her after she went to live with her father, and never invited her back home to visit. She seldom called to see how Germaine was.

Because she was so isolated from others while living with her father, Germaine became dependent on her father's girlfriends for her social life. "We would go to the movies and shopping," Germaine recalled. "They were pretty ladies, very feminine, real role models for me." Weren't these friendships awkward, I asked, considering that they were sharing the same man? "We just never spoke of it," Germaine said. "Sometimes I think it was actually a bond between us. We'd see an outfit in a men's shop that one of us would say would look good on him, and we'd both just giggle like crazy. I can't believe now how sick it was," she added, shaking her head. "Maybe that's how it is in polygamous marriages."

Then, Germaine's father had one of his girlfriends move in and share his bedroom on a permanent basis. "I tried being friends with her too," Germaine recalls, "but she wouldn't have it. She got mad if she saw me even talking to my dad and made him swear he'd never touch me again."

Germaine tried having friends outside the home, and eventually met and married a young man in the army while she was a senior in high school. This man looked remarkably like Germaine's father and treated her in much the same possessive yet rejecting way. He began cheating on her with other women ten years later, after their three children were born. Today, Germaine is married to a man who loves her, does not cheat on her, supports and loves her children, and will provide her with anything she needs. She came to therapy not because she had to escape yet another bad relationship, but because she found herself growing bored and restless and looking for a "bad" man with whom she could cheat on her husband.

"I know this can't be good," she said of these urges in her first therapy session. "I know I need to find out what's going on with me before I hurt the most wonderful man who ever lived and mess up the most wonderful marriage any woman could have."

Germaine has come to realize that she is feeling a compulsion to re-enact the "sins" of her father on another man and on her husband. She realizes, to her horror, that she was actually looking for a single dad she could steal away from his children with her sexual charms.

She understands now that the pattern of rejection by a stepmother and regaining love by using sex had become so powerful a force in her life that she had no use for the kind of everyday, consistent, reciprocal love her husband gave her. It's going to take her time and willpower to enjoy the love she has, but I feel sure she will do it. That's because she's the ideal therapy client—willing to do the work and willing to understand herself—willing to understand why she is like she is. She is also determined to spare her children, who love her husband as much as he loves them, the same kinds of pain she experienced when she was growing up.

11

Feeling Better

The following exercises are designed to counteract some of the bad feelings that can be caused by the kinds of mothers described in the foregoing chapters.

When you hate yourself and want to beat yourself up

These are common feelings in survivors of sexual abuse in childhood. When they strike, try doing the following:

1. Write your feelings in a journal (or on any paper you have handy).
2. Write a children's story. Start with the sentence, "Once upon a time there was a little girl who thought she was very bad. But she wasn't. So she...." And just keep going. Don't worry about grammar, spelling, or anything else.
3. Read a good children's book.
4. Play with some favorite possessions. You might set out your jewelry in circles or rows, arrange all your shoes in rows, or try on clothes you haven't worn in some time.

When you feel unbearably lonely

Survivor's loneliness can strike at any time, and it can be incapacitating. It makes you feel that you deserve to be alone, that no one wants you, and that you shouldn't even try to connect with anyone because no one wants to hear from you. Here are some ways to deal with such loneliness.

1. Find books you want to read. Books are instant company. (Making a "to read" list is a good idea.)

2. Compile reading matter for lonely times. It should not include magazines with photos of people who are obviously in happy relationships.

3. Find a list of organizations in your town—the Internet is a good resource—that need volunteers to work with people of various ages. Decide on the age group you want to work with, and contact a relevant group.

When you are addicted to people who are inherently destructive

Survivors of sexual abuse, incest, or rape are often attracted to destructive people. In all likelihood, you keep seeking them out and cannot relate to, or get interested in, "good" people who would treat you with respect. This problem can be serious. Here are some ways of dealing with it:

1. Make lists of the people you know who are helpful.

2. Make lists of all the ways these people are helpful.

3. Make lists of the benefits these people provide to you.

4. Make lists of the ways you can count on these people for things you need.

5. Make lists of the rules these people observe.

6. Make lists of the qualities these good people have that you would like your children to have.

When you don't want to do what you need to do

This common feeling can be very frightening. It's as though some force comes over you and keeps you from wanting to do what you need to do to get on in life, such as paying bills, keeping a dentist appointment, going to work, calling your boss to say you won't be coming to work, or keeping a promise to call an old friend. Here are some ways to combat this feeling:

1. Do one little piece at a time, like getting out your checkbook to write a check, finding a pen to write with, sitting at a table, and so on, until the check is written and the bill is stamped and mailed.
2. Let yourself feel good about doing every step.
3. Let yourself remember how guilty and worried you would have felt if you didn't fulfill the obligation.
4. Let yourself enjoy not feeling guilt, worry, and fear.
5. Make a list of things you accomplished, no matter how small, and check them off as you recall doing them.

When you get upset about self-care

Many survivors are taught to believe that they should not take care of themselves, that they are not worth their own or anyone else's protection and nurturing. As a result, many resist the most basic forms of self-care, such as bathing, grooming, cleaning their fingernails, and flossing their teeth. If you find yourself with this problem, try the following:

1. Pretend you are your own little girl. Give yourself a day of self-pampering.
2. Don't put yourself down if you neglect self-care.
3. List ways of nurturing your mind and body.
4. Make schedules for implementing these ways of nurturing.

5. Understand that the bad feelings you have about nurturing yourself aren't valid and you don't need to heed them.

6. List all the self-care tasks you enjoy doing.

When you hate your perpetrator and/or mother so much you can't stand it

This kind of rage is common in survivors and can be unexpected as well as incapacitating. When it strikes, try the following:

1. Let yourself feel the anger until it passes.

2. Tell yourself it's okay to feel this anger.

3. Tell yourself you have a right to feel this anger.

4. Let yourself enjoy the anger.

5. If the anger feels out of control, keeps escalating, and won't stop, visualize yourself putting it in a jar and putting a lid on it—temporarily. Then change your body position and think about something else.

PART TWO

LATE ADOLESCENT AND ADULT TRAUMA

12

The Mother's Role in Late Adolescent and Adult Trauma

This part of the book deals with adults who survived rape by acquaintances or strangers. I am not saying that the survivors' mothers enabled the perpetrators; the mothers never knew these rapists. I am saying that the mothers' roles in these survivors' lives appear to have made them vulnerable to rape and sexual assault.

In my work, I see about a third as many survivors of sexual trauma in adulthood as I do survivors of sexual trauma in childhood. At first, I assumed these clients had been relatively happy in childhood and in their lives until the sexual assault occurred. But in every case I found issues with the mother that caused the client to feel demeaned from early childhood on. Before moving on to the case histories, let's examine unwanted sexual activities.

What is sexual assault?

A sexual assault can be any act that forces a person to endure sexual penetration against his or her will. It can range from date rape to acquaintance rape to the most brutal kind of stranger rape, such as that described in *Lucky*, author Alice Seebold's novel about her rape.

What is sexual harassment?

Sexual harassment (unwanted sexual attention—especially after you've made it clear that you don't want it) can be as mild as "dirty talk" by someone who assumes that you will listen to it without asking if you want to listen to it (or goes ahead anyway, knowing that you don't want to hear it), to exposure of genitals without asking if you want to see them.

What is sexual molestation?

Sexual molestation is unwanted touching or fondling of breasts or genitals. Molestation can appear spontaneously, out of the blue, and often follows seemingly innocent physical contact, such as a pat on the back or a hug.

All of these forms of unwanted sexual contact can cause PTSD symptoms of various types and intensities. (For the sake of convenience, I'll refer to harassment, molestation, and assault as sexual assault from now on.)

At the end of the case histories, two chapters address getting help for symptoms caused by sexual assault. One chapter consists of quizzes designed to help you decide whether or not sexual assault is still affecting you and how serious your symptoms might be. The other chapter tells you where to go for help for your symptoms and how to tell if the help you find is what you need.

Now, on to the case histories.

CARA

Cara's mother led her to believe that she was so unappealing that she had to do whatever men wanted if she was to get a boyfriend.

Cara is a beautiful woman of 28 with carefully layered and streaked blonde hair, a toned, liposuctioned, augmented body, and a carefully planed and sculpted face and neck. When complimented on her appearance, Cara said she had "everything done" she could afford, "no more, really, than any woman would get done." What she meant, I discovered, was "no more" body enhancements than any of her friends or her mother would have had "done." "If we can enhance ourselves in any way, we'll try to do it," Cara added with a smile. At least her lovely smile was not "enhanced," but completely natural.

Cara came to see me because two men had recently sexually assaulted her. Both were men she met in dating bars; both were extremely good looking—"how a man looks is so important to me"; and both were relatively unknown to her when they assaulted her.

Both assaults happened within a month. The first occurred on a date with a man Cara was very attracted to. "It was our first real date," Cara said. "We'd been flirting in the bar for a couple of months and I was so happy when he asked me out." After dinner and drinks at an upscale restaurant, this man asked Cara if she wanted to see his apartment. "I said I would—I was dying to get in bed with him by that time."

But instead of the passionate experience Cara had expected, the sex became violent as soon as "we were in his apartment and he had shut and locked his front door." The man pushed Cara onto his couch, where he raped her forcefully twice, then dragged her into his bedroom where he raped her again three more times. Afterward, when Cara could barely move and was bleeding profusely, he asked her if she had enjoyed it. "Can you imagine? He thought I liked it." Cara reported him to the police the next day.

The police, unfortunately, were not helpful. "The detective I talked to said I brought it on myself by going out with him in the first place and dressing in an 'enticing' way. God, I was so mad."

About three weeks later, just as Cara was thinking she could put her date rape behind her, she went through a similar experience with another man she had been talking with at another bar. "He and I were good buddies," Cara said. "I told him about my rape and he was so sympathetic. He asked me if I wanted to go to a movie with him and promised he wouldn't try to do anything."

But after the movie, he assaulted Cara in his car—with a gun barrel. "He was a security guard for apartment complexes. We were still parked in the parking lot of the movie theater and he asked me if I wanted to see his gun. As it happens, I am interested in guns; I have gone shooting with my dad since I was a little girl. So he takes out his gun—a .45—and the next thing I know he's jamming the gun into me and saying that that's something he always wanted to do to a girl and he wanted to know how it felt. I got this sense that I had better pretend to enjoy it if I wanted to stay alive. That was truly even worse than the other rape because I was sure the gun was loaded and he had gone completely out of his mind."

After she pretended to be enjoying what this man did, he drove her home and promised "more fun" on the next date. When he called her again, Cara told him she had reconnected with an old boyfriend and was engaged. Luckily, he appeared to believe her and "wished me the best. Can you imagine? He didn't think there was a thing wrong with what he did."

Cara was afraid to report this rape to the police. "I know they would have said it was my fault for getting in the same situation again, and I couldn't go through that." But, thanks to the crisis advocate she spoke with after the second rape, Cara did agree to come in to see a therapist.

Only after weeks of therapy did she decide that meeting men in bars and only going out with the ones who were good looking might not be the safest practices.

This realization was difficult for Cara, because she was very happy with her social life before the rapes. She loved coming home from her secretarial job, dressing to the nines, putting on makeup for an hour, and then curling her hair strand by strand for another hour. Then she would pick up a girlfriend, who was as carefully dressed and groomed as she was, and go to a favorite bar, attracting the attention of all the males and choosing the best-looking ones to flirt with.

Cara loved spending her weekends hanging out with friends at the mall, shopping, going to a film, and then going out Saturday night for the big date of the week. "I felt like I'd achieved a lifestyle I always wanted and it was so much fun." She studiously ignored the facts that her job had no meaning for her other than providing a paycheck and that in about five years she would be too old for the bar scene. (She confided that she was already feeling in competition for men's attention with women five to seven years younger, not to mention the college-student cocktail waitresses.) Getting ready and going out again always enabled her to forget the less pleasant realities of her life.

But the rapes put an end to the life she enjoyed so much. Suddenly, Cara was having post traumatic stress disorder symptoms that rendered her terrified of the men she met in bars, terrified of being touched by a man—any man, even her dad—and unable to relax in bars without having enough drinks to "practically pass out from." She was so terrified of going to sleep in her apartment that she stayed up most of the night. She was so easily startled that she could no longer relax enough to flirt, and she was so subject to flashbacks of both rapes when she was at work, trying to sleep, and at other unexpected and inconvenient moments, that she was constantly agitated.

I didn't say to Cara, "Well, what can you expect, dressing up like a stripper, going to places full of men you don't know, and taking risks by being alone with them in their cars and apartments? Never, ever do these things again!" Instead, I helped her discover the feelings that had led her to go to singles bars so compulsively, and that led her to judge a man's worth only by his looks and surface personality.

At first she resisted, saying she didn't want to talk about anything she felt—she just wanted to make the PTSD symptoms go away so she could get back to her "normal" life, and that it was stupid to think she was any different from any other "girl" her age. (She almost always referred to herself as a "girl," or sometimes a "lady," never a "woman.")

But after three therapy sessions, Cara realized how angry she was at her mother's reaction to her rapes. She also got in touch with the deep rage at her mother that she had been trying to repress for years.

Cara's mother told Cara that she was to blame for the rapes. But then, Cara said, her mom had always told her that she was to blame for almost everything. When Cara was younger, she told her mom that none of the boys at school liked her. Her mother's reaction? She told Cara it was her fault for not being pretty. When Cara's mother's new husband didn't want Cara coming to visit, her mom told Cara it was her fault, because she didn't "act right" around him.

In therapy, Cara began to understand that her mother probably saw her as competition and that she would never be good enough for her mother, never worthy of her mother's love. An especially poignant memory was that of the time Cara "snared" (her word) her first "really great-looking, hunky boyfriend" and brought him home like a trophy to show to her mother. "You know what she said?" Cara asked me, her eyes brimming with tears, "She said to me right in front of him that he was gorgeous, but I wasn't pretty enough to hold onto him. Then she winked at this boy! God, she was flirting with him! I see that now."

Cara eventually realized that one of her main goals was proving she could hold on to a good-looking man, and so she wouldn't allow herself to be attracted to a man who wasn't magazine-model handsome. She would try, if the less-than-perfect-looking men were nice, to be sexually interested in them. But "the chemistry just wouldn't be there. They always ended up being friends."

Cara saw that holding these subconscious feelings and goals made her very vulnerable to being raped.

Meanwhile, Cara desperately wanted her mom to soothe and comfort her. "I always just wanted her to be a mom and say I was okay," Cara said one day in therapy, weeping copiously. "That's why I try to look so good!" She continued, "My mother always finds fault with the way I look when I don't have every eyelash curled and every hair in place, and I show so much as an ounce of being overweight."

After about a year of therapy, Cara's PTSD symptoms began to subside. She gave up hoping that her mother would ever change and become the mom she needed. She met a man on a blind date who was "not perfect" and to whom she was not sexually attracted. But she liked this man so much she decided to "make myself feel sexy with him." To this end, Cara planned a big seduction scene in her apartment complete with wine and cheese and the right music. It worked, she reported. The "sex was strange at first because I was forcing myself to respond. But then I started liking it, and it was great!" Cara and this man soon became engaged.

When Cara stopped therapy, she and her fiancé were planning a trip to his hometown so she could meet his family. Cara did take her fiancé to meet her mother, but warned her mother not to say one judgmental word about this man.

Clearly, Cara's mother had instilled attitudes and beliefs in her that predisposed Cara to being raped. She not only lacked a reliable values system for judging men, but she lacked that sense of radar that tells most women when a man is dangerous.

Looking back, Cara said there were red flags with both perpetrators. The first one had told her he was "into rough sex," but "ever wanting to seem sophisticated, I pretended not to react." The second man had told her "a little too often" how women thought his weapon was "really sexy."

But she did not allow herself to think such remarks disturbing. "The truth is, the things these men said did worry me—but I thought that was because I was just naive and I should be more sophisticated, like they were."

Cara's mother did not allow her to have her own thoughts about men—she was raised to have her mother's opinions of men. She was supposed to want a certain type of man, the "pretty boy," as Cara put it, the man who would turn heads in restaurants and bars. Cara's mother taught her not only to judge a man by his looks, but to desire men for their looks.

Cara's mother neglected to tell her that men who spend a great deal of their time and money on themselves may be narcissistic or sociopathic. Cara's mother also neglected to tell Cara that she should consider herself a kind and loving "good catch" the men would be lucky to win.

Instead, Cara's mother implied that Cara was not pretty enough to get and keep a really good-looking man, and should therefore feel grateful when one of them showed her attention. Her mother taught her that she should be ready to do whatever he wanted her to do, putting aside her discomfort and fears.

ANA

Ana, a beautiful woman in her forties, came to therapy because an unknown assailant brutally raped her in the alley outside the women's shelter where she was staying. She was on her way home from a job interview in a restaurant and "was a little scared, because it was night." Her perpetrator jumped out from the alley and dragged Ana back into it, duct taping her mouth shut as he did so. Then, not six feet from where she lived, he slowly tortured Ana with a cigarette lighter and raped her. "I was sure he would kill me," she said.

But then the perpetrator jumped up and fled, startled by a drug user who had come into the alley to use crack cocaine. The crack user helped Ana get home to the shelter, where staff called an ambulance. Ana spent the next 48 hours in a hospital.

Ana's mother had brought Ana up to believe that she was unlovable and ugly. "She hated me for some reason. I think I reminded her of her own mother in the way I looked and acted. She never said a kind word to me, ever, just to the other kids." Yet, paradoxically, Ana's mother also instilled the belief in Ana that she had to get a husband or suffer a terrible life.

"I left home at 15 with the first man who wanted to marry me." Ana replaced this husband with five others as she tried in vain to find a man who would "treat me well and not abuse me."

In therapy, Ana got in touch with her feelings about her mother. She realized how much her mother's opinion of her as a little girl had formed her opinion of herself as a victim in need of a man. She also saw how vulnerable this desperation for a man had made her.

I don't want to imply that Ana's mother caused her to be in the alley where she was raped. That is not the case. But, I believe, her treatment of Ana had an indirect influence on Ana's assault. Ana's mother had instilled in Ana the insecurity and low self-esteem that led her to being abandoned, broke, and staying in a shelter in a dangerous neighborhood.

JUDY

When Judy came for therapy, she was a toothless woman in her early forties who was seeking help for two reasons: she was having flashbacks of her married life, which consisted of frequent sexual assault by her husband and his biker friends; and she was unable to be intimate with her new husband.

Judy's married life had consisted of 18 years of working daytimes as a nursing aide and working evenings to sexually service her husband's friends, in exchange for cash and drugs. Her husband would beat Judy if she didn't perform well and he didn't get his drugs. Judy implied that a no-questions-asked dentist in Mexico had pulled her teeth so that she could better perform oral sex. That memory was so painful that she couldn't recall it directly without reacting hysterically, so she would only allude to it indirectly.

Why, you might ask at this point, did Judy remain in this situation when she could have escaped any time during the day? The simple reason is that Judy's husband threatened her with bodily harm and probably murder if she tried to escape. The underlying reason is that her mother told her she did not deserve decent treatment by a man.

Judy's current husband had been a frequent guest at Judy's husband's orgies, but had been unable to join in the sexual abuse. "Instead, he would always whisper when it was his turn to have sex with me that he was going to get me out of there and that he had real feelings for me."

One day, this man came to see Judy where she worked and told her to come to his house that night, and to file for divorce the next day. Though terrified that her husband would get revenge on them both, Judy followed his suggestions and was divorced within six months. Her soon-to-be ex-husband had "a new old lady to show off within two weeks," Judy said. "He met her at a biker bar."

Meanwhile, flashbacks and other PTSD symptoms kept Judy from being able to enjoy sex with a new husband who cared about her and treated her well. Though he was patient and willing to wait, he was eager for Judy to get over her symptoms so she could enjoy life again.

He had his own problems, too. He had done time in prison for drug dealing and was having trouble finding a job, thanks to his felony charge. But despite their problems, the couple was determined to have a good married life. Both were from ostensibly "respectable, good families" and knew they could do better than they had.

Upon working with Judy in therapy, however, I found that her "respectable, good" family had treated her in ways that predisposed her to marrying a man like her abusive ex-husband. "I just wanted to get out of the house, and I didn't care who wanted to marry me, just so he'd give me another roof over my head," Judy recalled.

Judy had been the victim in childhood not of actual physical abuse but of astonishing physical and emotional neglect. From the time she was a little girl, her mother had pushed Judy aside as though she did not exist. She never had a room of her own, was forced to sleep in corners of the house on the floor, and was left by herself for hours and sometimes days by parents who worked all day and sometimes went off for weekends without letting any of their children know they were going. Judy's two much older brothers did have a bedroom of their own and often went off by themselves when their parents were gone. Or, when they were older, the brothers would have friends over for beer parties, during which Judy would cower in a closet so they would not notice her and "maybe do something bad to [her]."

Judy has no idea why her mother treated her this way. "I was born to her late in life and maybe that had something to do with it," Judy said. A few times CPS took her away from her family because a relative or teacher had reported her neglect. "I loved those times because I'd be paid attention to and given a real bed to sleep on." But, for reasons Judy doesn't understand to this day, CPS always returned her to her family. "I suppose my mother would promise to do better with me. I don't really know."

As she grew older, Judy settled into a state of constant despair and depression. "I had clothes brought in boxes by my mother who I guess got them from thrift stores. I wasn't starving because I knew to get myself food from the refrigerator and I'd be given a plate after every-one else was finished eating." But her parents completely ignored her needs for communication and affection. "My mother would talk to other people but never, ever to me. It was just so weird."

It may sound like Judy was making all this up. But after reading her CPS record and speaking to a worker familiar with her case, I found out that she was not making anything up. The conditions reported by CPS workers were those she described to me.

Judy met her ex-husband through her brothers—both of whom eventually became substance abusers who spent time in and out of prison. When her ex-husband first took a "liking" to her, he was able to get Judy to do anything he wanted. "I was so thrilled that somebody liked me." She had by then dropped out of school.

Somewhere along the way of her more and more horrifying life, Judy got a GED and a nurse's aide certification. She enjoyed her job caring for patients in nursing homes. "It was so nice being around nice people who needed me every day. I used to lie to them and tell them my husband was a schoolteacher and took me out to dinner every night."

In reality, Judy's husband was unemployed except for drug dealing and committing violent acts for pay. He mostly got support from Judy, who paid the rent, the utilities, the food bills, and the tab from the biker bar he frequented without her.

The question of why Judy endured this treatment has the same answer as the question of why she endured the neglect from her parents. Her parents had led her to believe that she didn't merit better treatment and deserved what she got. "It wasn't that my mom said I was bad, just not worth treating good," Judy said in therapy, her eyes brimming with tears.

What did Judy's mother do all those years when Judy was a child? She lived a life largely separate from her children. Judy's mother was more involved with Judy's brothers, but these boys ran roughshod over their parents. "They just had the run of the house. I don't think Mom cared. She spent a lot of time putting on makeup, talking to friends on the phone, watching TV, going out to lunch and girls' nights out with her friends. Mom always looked great. She'd yell at me to comb my hair sometimes, but never ever combed or washed it for me that I can remember." Judy recalls that her mother's parents spoiled her mom but also ignored Judy. "It was like Mom never grew up in her own mind or anyone else's."

It does indeed sound like Judy's mom remained a child—a spoiled, pampered little girl. Her dislike of anyone who might threaten that status, including her own child, made her deny that child's existence. When Judy later told her mother what she was going through in her marriage, her mom told her not to think of coming back home. "She never cared that I married my husband. She said we had to elope because she wasn't having any wedding, so we did. And she didn't care what he did to me after we were married, not once."

Needless to say, Judy has ceased all contact with her parents and has never introduced them to her second husband. "I did spend time with them a few years ago when they were sick and needed me to nurse them. But I won't do it again because they told me when I did take care of them I had to pay them for any food I ate."

MARGARET

Margaret's mother was the opposite of Judy's, at least in her mothering. She "fussed over me like I was her little doll," Margaret recalled in therapy. "She curled my hair, ironed every ruffle on every dress and gave me little bracelets and necklaces with the sweetest charms."

Margaret came in for therapy when she was 27 because of a rape by a friend of a friend who "came on to me in this real romantic way, then raped me." A successful and beloved schoolteacher, Margaret had nevertheless been unable to find a boyfriend throughout her life, and had welcomed this man's advances. "He seemed so nice. I just never thought he'd do what he did."

Beset with PTSD symptoms when she came to therapy, especially a fear of men, Margaret was also depressed. "It's hard enough not having a boyfriend and having to face being an old maid without being afraid now that every man will hurt me in some way."

In therapy, Margaret decided to work on her difficulty establishing a relationship with a man. In the process, she recalled her mother saying to her when she was a child that "You're only good enough for me, you're our little girl."

Margaret remembers saying, "I'll never leave you and Daddy, Mommy," and asking if it would be possible for her to marry Daddy, when she got old enough to do so.

During her later childhood, Margaret's mother began finding things wrong with her. "My looks were never quite right, my grades never high enough, my friends never quite nice enough, and my room never quite clean enough. I'd try to be better at whatever I wasn't doing perfectly and sometimes I'd succeed." But the idea of being naturally attractive to someone else, as she was, was unthinkable to Margaret. She began to have crushes on boys from afar, always hoping one of them would reciprocate. Her parents would not allow her to go out with other kids in a crowd, so she didn't learn how to socialize with boys. They sometimes allowed her to have a friend over for a sleepover or to go with a friend to the movies or to a church event. But her mother refused to allow anything more.

Margaret got through high school, college, and teachers' training feeling like a nun with a calling. "I just wanted to be a good teacher and make my mom proud." She had no idea how much she missed having a boyfriend until her perpetrator came on to her. "We were sitting in the park on a bench when he told me he really liked me and started giving me little kisses. Before I knew it, he was leading me to his car and into his back seat, and that's where he raped me."

The attention and the touching felt "so good," Margaret finally admitted in therapy, "that I didn't know what I was doing."

Margaret came to realize in therapy that her mother never allowed her to have an identity of her own. She was always her mom's little doll—"her Franklin Mint doll," Margaret said with a laugh. "She had those dolls all over the house." The refusal of this mother to accept Margaret as a separate person with her own developing identity undermined Margaret's sense of self in ways she could not repair. Only her mother could give her the seal of approval she craved—and that the mother refused to do.

Now, Margaret sees herself as a complete person with imperfections. She is working on not having to be perfect and on relating to others, especially men, as people with their own personalities. She is also learning to trust her intuition about men so she'll be less vulnerable to a man who treats her as the sweet little doll her mother always told her she was.

NITA

I realize that saying a mother "made" a daughter a magnet for rape is a strong statement. Mental health professionals tell clients that no one can "make" them do anything. But in Nita's case, her mother did exactly that.

Nita's mother has been telling Nita she was "a slut" since Nita was old enough to remember. The mother, whom I once met in the lobby of my office, is tall and angular, with straight hair. Nita is curvaceous with naturally curly hair. The mother is hard, unsmiling, and assertive in her manner, while Nita is naturally soft, sweet, and quick to laugh. From what Nita says about her mother, it seems clear that her mother has always considered Nita's feminine qualities sinful and dangerous.

As a child, Nita was very religious. She spent every spare moment in church, assisting the nuns and studying religion with the priests. She can't remember if any of them ever molested her, and she has absolutely no memory of the details of her service to the church.

When she was a teenager, Nita's mother was always yelling at her for being a temptress. "I dressed the way all the girls dressed in my school, but she said I was a slut."

Nita lived in fear of her body, her looks, and her normal sexual feelings during all of her teenage years. She withdrew socially and dedicated herself to studying, so she could become a teacher. Being bilingual, she felt that she would have no trouble getting a job. At sixteen, she became attracted to a boy who was "a bad boy," a gang member and drug dealer. She had a secret affair with him for about a year, and felt totally addicted to him. "It was like I was finally being what my mother always said I was, and it was fun," Nita said. "But I always felt so guilty and afraid she would find out I wanted to die."

When she was seventeen, Nita got pregnant and had to tell her mother. The result was an abortion that her mother said would send her to hell, and then regular beatings from her mother for the next two years. Nita now knew that her mother was right, that she was intrinsically bad, that just by existing she would attract other bad people and tempt good people to sin. Being pretty and feminine was a dangerous way to be, Nita decided, not just for herself but for other innocent people as well.

Thoroughly depressed, Nita lived a monastic, celibate life. She was her mother's helper around the house and in her mother's flourishing private nursing practice. "I kept her books, I organized her office and answered the phone. If I did good, she left me alone. If I did something wrong she ranted and raved. My reward for doing a good job was to be spared the verbal attacks."

By the time she graduated from high school, Nita felt so apathetic about life that she didn't even apply for college. "Besides," she said, "I was afraid I would seduce all the other students, the teachers I worked with and, God forbid, the students I taught."

Then, one day when she was 21, Nita saw a sign on an adult nightclub saying, "Girls wanted. Make $500 a day." Overcome with the thought of having financial freedom, Nita applied for the job and was hired immediately. "I didn't have any guilt at all about stripping," she said. "I was already considered bad, so why not make money at it." Nita moved out of her mother's house with her first paycheck, ignoring her mother's horror and warnings that she would now be in real danger.

A little over a month later, a customer followed her home to her apartment, forced himself inside when she unlocked the door, and raped her. She reported the rape to the police, quit her job, and moved back home. Within a few months, however, she could no longer endure her mother's abuse and was back working in another strip club. But flashbacks and other PTSD symptoms from her rape prevented her from being able to hold that job for long.

When Nita came for therapy, she believed I would tell her that she deserved to suffer because she was so sinful. She was surprised to learn that I considered her to be a normal woman with normal sexual appetites. Nita got in touch with her feelings about her mother and her mother's messages that she must be very good all the time or she would become very bad. Nita realized that an in-between state of being existed that involved trying to be responsible and now and then being tempted to be a bit bad, but maybe not acting on that impulse. She saw that she could decide what she wanted to do, date men who were good people, and earn money in jobs that didn't exploit her sexually and make her vulnerable to sexual assault.

After about a year of therapy, Nita was finally able to go to college, detach from her mother, and begin a new life. She is now working in a clerical job, is in a college she loves, and is enjoying friendships with other students who are respectful of her.

Nita's mother has been furious with Nita, with me, and with our agency for not inflicting upon Nita the kind of suffering-and-repentance therapy she thinks Nita needs.

But Nita has been able to ignore her mother's angry phone calls. She is thinking of getting a restraining order against her mother if her mother continues showing up in her dorm room on campus at all hours, yelling at Nita for not living at home.

Getting away from her mother and her mother's attitude toward her body and her femininity has given Nita the self-esteem and freedom she needs to do well. It's also given her the ability to keep herself out of situations that are likely to lead to sexual assault.

Clearly, Nita's mother has had competition and desire issues with Nita from the time Nita was born. The desire issues might well have escalated as Nita's beauty developed.

Am I saying a mother can desire her own daughter? Yes—any parent can desire a child, just as any human being can desire any other human being. I believe that Nita's mother blamed Nita for being attractive to her, so she made Nita ashamed of her own sexuality. As a result of this shame, Nita felt compelled to work in a strip club. She felt she deserved the leers and disrespect, and even the sexual assault, of the customers, because of the way she was.

When a mother tells her daughter she is nothing more than a sexual object, that mother is making her daughter vulnerable to rape. The daughter believes the mother is right, that her attractiveness is proof she is a "bad" girl who tempts men to sin. And then, believing her mother is right about her sinfulness, she acts out that sinfulness by working in strip clubs and getting into other situations sure to provide the disrespect from men she thinks she deserves.

13

Lessons from the Case Histories

I do not mean to suggest that your mother, or anyone else, can protect you from rape. This is simply not true. Many people who have caring, nurturing mothers have been raped by "friends," acquaintances, and strangers.

But I do believe that the mothers described in the preceding case histories made their daughters vulnerable to rape. How? They failed to instill in the survivors that special inbuilt "radar" that helps protect women from sexual assault. This "radar" is a sense of self-preservation that is always "on," that operates in the most normal of situations.

Here's an example of that radar at work: I was in the post office about 15 years ago on a hot summer day, smiling and chatting with other people about the weather and the possibility of rain. Since I was riding my bike, I had more than a passing concern about the rain.

Suddenly I saw a man looking at me in a way that made me very alert. There was nothing unusual about him: he was nicely dressed, in his middle thirties, clean-shaven, and with a stylish haircut. But he was looking at me in a focused, predatory way that kicked my "fight or flight" response system into high gear. I was somewhat, but not entirely, relieved when he turned and left the p.o. before I did.

When I left the post office, I looked for him in the parking lot but didn't see him. But as I was riding my bike down the street, I realized that a car was driving slowly behind me, following me. A quick turn of my head set off alarms: the driver was the man in the post office. I rode my bike up to a house—having no idea who lived there but wanting to have the man think I lived there—and he drove by. When no one answered my frantic knocks, I turned away—and saw the vehicle begin to back up. He had stopped his car up the street and watched to see if I went into the house.

Frantic, I ran across the street and pounded on the door of another house. This time, a woman let me in and, miraculously, believed my story about being followed. She let me call the police and my husband. When she and I went outside to wait for my husband, who was coming to pick me up in our truck, the same man was driving by again. In one sense, I was relieved. Now I could prove this man really did exist. But in another sense, it was more terrifying than ever. I realized I was still being stalked. A predator, this man had been willing to interrupt his day and stalk his prey in the nicest of neighborhoods—and I had known it. The expression in his eyes when I first saw him told me everything. Had I ignored that expression, and the feelings it evoked in me, I might be dead today. Just writing about that experience brings back the fear and panic I felt then. Luckily, I was able to trust my intuition, and my intuition saved me.

The clients I discuss in this part of the book grew up not only not trusting their intuition, but believing their intuition, indeed, their every feeling, every need, every natural desire, was flawed. It's no wonder they had no way to tell who was a potential rapist and who wasn't.

How exactly did their mothers set these clients up for rape?

• The negative attitudes their mothers had toward them made these clients needy for love—physical love, emotional love, approving love, nurturing love, rejoice-in-the-child's-being love. It's no wonder they completely trusted any man who demonstrated any of these kinds of love, even for a moment. The loving felt so good! As one client said, "I just loved the way he [her perpetrator] seemed to like me—no one had ever liked me that much before, no one."

• The clients were too exhausted mentally and emotionally to protect themselves. Growing up with the mothers they did forced them into exercising a kind of self-control that others find hard to relate to. It's self-control that is never relaxed. Trying hard is the watchword of their lives from the time they are very young, and trying hard requires self-control. These clients have to try hard to make up for the innate qualities they possess that trigger their mothers to hate them. They have to try hard to repress their anger at their mothers for abusing them emotionally and physically. They have to try hard not to act like the bad girls their mothers say they are. They have to try hard not to have natural, spontaneous fun because it makes their mothers angry. They have to worry all the time about relaxing their iron self-control, because they know that if they do they will become sluts, bad girls, and heaven knows what other things their mothers said they would become. No wonder these clients sometimes drink or use drugs to medicate away their exhausted feelings and depression and/or to pump themselves up to try even harder.

• Clients needed excessive affirmation of their gender identities. A woman who is not sure that being a woman is "a good thing," as Martha Stewart puts it, will fail to be as protective of herself as a woman who loves being a woman and knows it is a wonderful thing. None of the mothers in the foregoing cases made their daughters feel good about being female. And none presented a happy role model as a woman. The clients feared that their genders alone made them bad people. As such, they were not worth protecting from risk. If a man offered any affirmation of their gender at all, they would trust him completely in the hope that the gender affirmation would continue.

The willingness to take unreasonable risks is so prevalent in clients who are rape survivors that it still amazes me.

The needs of my clients for all the good feelings that their mothers denied them made them more willing to take risks than they should have been. They were more willing than other women to go to a strange man's apartment, to let a strange man buy them drinks in a bar, to get too intimate too soon with a man they didn't know, to go out alone very late at night, or to indulge in strange sex practices even when these practices repulsed them. I will never hold these clients accountable for doing these risky things, because I know why they were taking such risks.

If you find yourself taking similar risks, please get therapy immediately so that you can get your needs for love and care met by someone who can really help you instead of by someone who might do you harm.

14

Are You Still Suffering from Your Sexual Assault?

Here's the thing about sexual assault: If you don't get therapy for it, you usually don't get over it. You can experience symptoms of PTSD—post traumatic stress disorder—for months or even years after you thought you were recovered. You might think you're not going to have any symptoms and then, suddenly, boom! Fifteen years after the assault you can start experiencing one of more PTSD symptoms big time, without any warning at all. What I'm telling you now is documented, but it's also apparent in all of my clients.

Here, in brief, are the most common symptoms of PTSD:

• **Panic attacks**. A panic attack is a feeling of sudden panic, often leading to the fear of not being able to breathe and of losing consciousness. A panic attack is incapacitating until it passes. You just have to sit down and wait it out.

• **Terror of being attacked again**. You are constantly vigilant, always looking to see who is around you, and you are easily startled. The least little thing can make you jump and sometimes scream out loud.

• **Recurring nightmares**. The same nightmare comes over and over, sometimes making you afraid to go to sleep at night. One of my clients has dreamed every night for years that she is being held and paralyzed by an unseen force, and prevented from waking up even though she knows she is dreaming. Another has dreams filled with feces in stopped-up toilet. Gorillas attack her in another of her recurring dreams.

- **Flashbacks**. These are movies that you suddenly find yourself watching while you are awake. The images in these movies are often violent and can be a replay of a violent aspect of your sexual trauma. They can last up to ten minutes and render you absolutely incapacitated until they are over. Flashbacks come on without any warning, right in the middle of meetings, sexual encounters, and in other settings where they are especially unwelcome.

- **Irritability**. You find yourself lashing out at people you like and even love over little things that shouldn't bother you at all, let alone cause a major meltdown. You find that you have no patience with anyone– and no appreciation of people's honest efforts to do their best.

- **Insomnia**. You might be able to fall asleep after tossing and turning in bed for hours, then find yourself wide awake an hour later. You may get very tired during the day or in the evening, when you're supposed to be alert, but find yourself unable to go into the sleep state if you try to take a nap.

Other PTSD symptoms exist, but these are the ones I encounter most often in my clients.

You need to get help for these symptoms. Why? Because, if not treated, these symptoms can be retriggered. Anything that reminds you of the assault, in any way, can have you going through the whole thing all over again—the fear, the flashbacks, the anger outbursts, the nightmares. This reminder can be as simple as a touch by someone you love or as brutal as a news story detailing a rape.

I have two clients whose symptoms re-emerged ten years after they were assaulted. A TV show about a feminist performance artist who adorns herself in simulated feces triggered one client. The other was triggered by a beloved new boyfriend touching her intimately.

Many of my clients did get counseling soon after they were sexually assaulted. But the counseling was usually short term, geared toward making the client "put the whole thing behind [her] as soon as possible," as one client put it, and toward providing more comfort than therapy. This kind of treatment helps the client bury the symptoms and get on with her life—but the buried symptoms can reappear at any time.

For now, please take the following quizzes. They might help you understand your feelings about your sexual assault. Even if you have not been sexually assaulted as an adult, but just as a child, you will find these quizzes informative. All of the questions are derived from actual symptoms experienced by clients who survived sexual assault.

Love life

Have you ever . . . ? Write Yes, No, or DR (for "Don't Remember") after every question.

- felt panic when someone you loved touched you?
- felt repulsed when someone you loved touched you?
- felt fear when someone you loved touched you?
- felt fear when having to sleep against the wall?
- felt loathing when someone you loved indicated he or she wanted to be sexual?
- said you had a headache or nausea when someone you cared about wanted to be playful?
- felt under attack if your partner wanted anything except straight sex?
- experienced a flashback to your sexual assault during lovemaking?
- felt relief when your partner was too tired to make love?
- felt relief when your partner was going to be away for a few days and you wouldn't have to be amorous?
- felt fear because your partner was going to be away for a few days and you would be alone?
- felt angry because your partner didn't care that you didn't want sex, but wanted it anyhow?
- felt angry because your partner was not affectionate and caring enough?
- been reminded of your sexual assault when you had erotic feelings?

- felt a need to talk about your rapist nonstop to your partner, making him or her listen even if he or she doesn't want to?
- felt that your partner was prying and intrusive if he or she wanted to know the details of your assault?
- felt that your partner didn't care about you if he or she didn't want to hear about your assault?
- felt disgusted by sex, all parts of it?
- felt like damaged goods that no nice person would want?

Work life

Have you ever . . . ? Again, write Yes, No, or DR after the questions.

- wished that your job was all you had to do in life?
- wanted your boss to stop looking at you in a certain way?
- wanted your boss to stop touching you in a certain way?
- wished that co-workers would not hug you?
- wished that co-workers and your boss would not ask you questions about your private life?
- wished that your co-workers would leave you alone?
- wished that your co-workers would mind their own business?
- wished that your co-workers could understand what happened to you?
- wished that your co-workers didn't leave you alone so much?
- felt unclean with your co-workers?
- felt like someone not worthy of being with your co-workers?

Mental symptoms

This section will help you assess the extent of such normal after-assault symptoms as flashbacks, outbursts of anger, irritability, and nightmares.

Have you ever . . . ? Write Yes, No, or Maybe after every question.

- been forced to "relive" a memory of your assault involuntarily in a flashback?
- had nightmares about your assault?
- felt like you were having more bad dreams than usual?
- felt like you didn't want to go to sleep because you would have bad dreams?
- felt that you had to tell people close to you about your sudden reliving of your assault (flashbacks), because you wanted them to understand why you behaved weirdly (were unable to focus because you were seeing the "memory movie" in your mind) and could not help what was happening to you?
- felt dread of these sudden memories when they started?
- been relieved when the memories ended?
- been afraid that people you love could become violent?
- been unusually jumpy?
- been afraid to be in a physical position you could not escape from quickly (such as having to sit in the back of a room near the wall)?
- been afraid to sit with your back to a door because you needed to be able to see who was coming in?
- been afraid to lie on the outside of the bed with your partner near the wall because you would be vulnerable to intruders?
- been afraid to lie on the inside near the wall with your partner on the outside because you would be trapped?

- been unreasonably angry with people you like over trivial matters?

- been unreasonably angry with your partner for wanting more affection than you wanted to give?

- been frequently irritable over trivial matters with people who love you?

- been afraid to face your perpetrator for fear that you would be out of control?

- been afraid that you could do harm to your perp in a way that would get you arrested?

- been afraid that you could ruin your life by acting on the rage you feel?

- been amazed at how much rage you feel?

- found yourself goading people to act in a way that justified your getting angry at them?

- found yourself looking for negative characteristics in people (such as jealousy, greed, competitiveness, and other qualities you dislike)?

- found yourself fearing that you are being stalked by someone?

- found that you are drawn to high risk situations (like going alone to grungy bars and wild parties) more than before the assault?

- found that you are suspicious of low-risk situations (such as being in nice restaurants with friends)?

- found that you are terrified for your children's safety in ways you never were before—such as when they go to visit a friend or leave your sight for any reason at all?

- found that you want to carry weapons, such as mace or even a gun?

- found that martial arts lessons now appeal to you in ways they never did before?

- found that you are not interested in any of your hobbies anymore?

- found that you can't enjoy trivial activities anymore, such as small talk with friends about clothes, interior décor, sports, or other inconsequential topics?
- found that you no longer care what others think of hairstyles, clothes, sports, cars, or other minor matters?
- found that you no longer want to share your opinions, thoughts and feelings about anything inconsequential?
- found that all you want to think and talk about are sexual assault laws and practices?

Social life

Have you ever . . . ? Write Yes, No, or DR after the questions.

- been uncomfortable at social gatherings in ways you weren't before your assault?
- felt that people you know who are the same gender as your perp now have ulterior motives toward you sexually?
- felt that your friends wanted you to "move on" and "get over" your sexual assault?
- felt that you were "unclean" compared to friends who had never been sexually assaulted?
- felt that your friends believed you caused the rape or sexual assault with your high-risk behavior—such as dressing in a certain way or being in a certain place at a certain time with certain people?
- felt that you can no longer connect with new people as well as you did before you were assaulted?
- wanted to tell every new person you met within five minutes of the introduction that you were raped?
- felt that friends of the same gender as the rapist were no longer safe or really worthy of your trust?

Relationship with your mother

Have you ever . . . ? Write Yes, No, or Maybe after the questions.

- felt that your mother blamed you for the rape?
- felt that your mother treated you less lovingly after the rape?
- felt that your mother wanted you to pretend that the rape never happened?
- felt that your mother was ashamed of you?
- felt that you let your mother down by getting raped?
- felt that you should apologize to your mother for getting raped?
- felt that your mother is no longer proud of you because you were raped?
- felt like "soiled goods" around your mother since your rape?
- felt a new, subtle coldness in your mother's attitude toward you since the rape?
- felt judged by your mother in some new way since you were raped?
- felt like a disappointment to your mother because of the rape?
- felt that on some deep level your mother suspects that you might have wanted to be raped?
- felt the loss of unconditional love from your mother because of the rape?
- felt that you now have to prove yourself to your mother in some way you didn't have to before your rape?
- felt that your mother no longer considers you a "good girl"?
- felt that you are no longer a good girl because of your mother's treatment of you?

Your relationship to yourself

Since your rape or sexual assault, have you ever . . . ? Write Yes, No, or Sometimes after the following questions.

- felt worthless?
- felt that you let yourself down?
- felt that you can't rely on your instincts?
- felt that your sexual needs are out of your control?
- felt that you attract evil people more than other people do?
- felt that you give the impression to others that you want to be "violated"?

Scoring

Add up your Nos, Yeses, Maybes and Don't Remembers. If you have more Yeses, Maybes and Don't Remembers than you have Nos, you can assume that you are still affected by your sexual assault. If you've already had counseling, you can assume that you need more. If you have not had any counseling, please try to find it.

Now, add up your scores in every category. The category in which you have the highest percentage of Yeses is the category in which you are especially affected.

If you need help, there are bound to be resources in your town that provide counseling at prices you can afford. Rape crisis centers abound in America, and they're easy to find. (Go to an Internet search engine and enter the keywords "rape crisis center" [in parentheses] and your city.) Get long-term psychotherapy, if at all possible. The advantages of long-term psychotherapy for adult survivors of sexual assault and rape are explained in detail in the next chapter.

What if you can't find therapy? Then look at the list of books in Appendix B and read at least one of them, whichever appeals to you most, several times. If you are comforted, soothed, and better informed with every reading, you'll know the reading is helping and in some ways healing you.

What to do right now

Here are things you can do to take care of yourself now, before finding therapy or counseling:

- Stop thinking you should have moved on and gotten over your sexual assault.
- Stop letting your mother's opinion of you matter.
- Stop feeling the assault was your fault in any way.
- Stop letting anyone, especially your mother, tell you how you feel about the assault.
- Stop making big decisions at this time, if you possibly can.
- Read the rest of this book.

PART THREE

PRESENT AND FUTURE

The following chapters deal with issues that either affect you now or could affect you in the future. Please read these chapters even if you don't think they're relevant to your situation.

15

Are you living with incest and rape?

Incest and rape can become such an accepted part of your life that you think enduring them is normal—at least for you.

Most people fail to realize that incest can go on—and on and on and on—for years on end. I have three clients whose incestuous relations with their fathers lasted until the clients were 18. I have clients whose every sexual encounter with husbands and significant others were rapes: forced sex with no foreplay, no seductiveness, no attempt whatsoever to make the experience fun.

If you're enduring either of these situations, don't beat yourself up about it. Don't feel guilty because you might enjoy it. Don't think that you can't get out of it, because you can. And, most of all, don't feel bad if you don't want to get out of it.

Let's look at these possibilities one at a time:

Feeling guilty because the incest and/or sexual assault is enjoyable

A client who had an affair with her father all through high school admits that he was a lover who gave her constant delight. She says she'd still be with him today, five years later, if he had not found another woman he liked better. "I was so jealous of her," my client said, "you can't imagine." This client is glad that she left her father, glad that the affair ended. "But sometimes I miss him sexually. Oh, God, can you believe what I just said?"

Of course I can. The sex was loving and nurturing and exquisite. My client was having a lot of sexual desire, as teenagers tend to have, and there was no one to suspect what was going on. Her mother had died in a car accident when she was 12, and her father had never remarried.

But then he didn't have to—he had his love interest right there at home.

I know of two brother-and-sister incest relationships that went on for years. In one of them, the brother fell so in love with his sister that he was never able to keep his marriages or other relationships alive. He would choose women as different from his sister in looks and behavior as possible, and then lose sexual and emotional interest in them. In the other relationship (which I believe is still continuing, although not as ardently as it once did, since both are now in their seventies) the sister became so dependent on the relationship to meet her needs that she never pursued another partner. The brother, in it mostly for the convenient sex (although he is fond of the sister in a brotherly way), is now living in a retirement home and enjoying the attentions of the many single women living there.

Another client, whose affair with her father lasted from the time she was seven until she was 18, is devastated at the loss of this lover. He is now in prison, having turned himself in, and my client desperately misses him. She was suicidal when she first came for therapy, because she felt totally alone. She missed her father terribly. She had also been rejected by her mother (who apparently really did have no idea what was going on, and was very angry when she found out) and her extended family, and she had rejected the counselor her aunt sent her to because the counselor told the aunt everything the client said in her sessions (a gross breach of ethics by the therapist). But she especially missed her father. He knew how to please her deliciously and had done so on a regular basis, several times a week, for many years. This incestuous relationship, too, would still be going on had the father not stopped it by turning himself in and being put in jail.

As for enjoying rape, any kind of sexual contact can be pleasurable, no matter how horrid it might seem. Spanking, bondage, torture —all can be sexually enjoyable as can other practices too numerous to name. One client said that she enjoyed being raped every night by her partner, because "it was the only way I can have sex. I had to pretend I didn't like it, though, and play victim because he had to pretend to be a rapist every time." The client who was raped by drunken bikers every night of her marriage never admitted to enjoying it. But I suspect she found some pleasure in it some of the time. A client who was regularly assaulted by an uncle as a child said she lived for those rare times her uncle felt like "being nice to me and would actually make love to me, instead of just f—— me without any thought of how much it hurt me."

Enjoyment of any kind of sex is never something to feel bad or guilty about. Our bodies are made to respond sexually. We all need sex of some kind.

Don't think you can't get out of these long-term relationships—because you can

You might feel trapped in the incestuous relationship. You might fear what will happen to the family structure if you stop the incestuous relationship. You might fear what will happen to your children or your source of support or your place to live if you get out of the partner-rape relationship. You might, in other words, feel that lots of people's well-being will suffer if you stop what's going on.

Please, please find a therapist to talk with about this situation. You can take charge of your own life and make a new one. But you will have a hard time doing so without help and support from someone who understands what's happening.

However, be prepared. If you are a minor child, your counselor or therapist will have to report the abuser to Child Protective Services. That's the law. If that scares you, realize that it's a good law and that what your abuser is doing is wrong.

Don't feel bad because you don't want to get out of the relationship

This relationship is what you know—you might be afraid that without it you'll be alone, a fate seemingly worse than death. Recently, a client whose partner raped her every night had him evicted by the police. It wasn't because she wanted to end the relationship, but because her partner threatened to "put a bullet through [her] head" and she knew he was dangerous, especially when drinking. But in spite of his abusiveness, his put downs, his refusal to show her any affection or respect, my client sorely misses him. "I just want him back," she cried out in my office last week. "I know it's crazy but I just want him back. I don't care what he did to me. I just want him to move back in." Then she dissolved into tears.

As of this writing, she is on a suicide watch. She told as many people as she could, including me, that she did not want to live if she couldn't have this man back.

Did I say to her, "Why on earth would you want him back after all the terrible ways he treated you"? No. I told her that she isn't "crazy" and that I was with her in her pain. I am worried about her, though, because I know that this relationship is her only relationship. She's never had the chance to make any new friendships that involve respectful treatment and love, not to mention respectful, pleasurable sex. And I know that she is as addicted to her abuser and what he gives her, in his angry, hurtful way, as others are to heroin.

Incest victims become addicted to their families in ways that normal people are not. This addiction happens partly because the survivor feels the incest was her fault and partly because she has a compulsive need to prove to her family that she is really "good," because then, she believes, she'll get the approval from them that she craves. No other family can bestow this approval, the victim believes, only the family associated with the incest.

If you are an adult, and your partner/perpetrator is an adult or your incest partner is an adult, you need to consider the following:

• The incestuous relationship is limiting your life. Think of all the people you can't get to know and the things you can't do because of it.

• The incestuous relationship is not contributing to your personal growth. When parents and/or siblings are also lovers, they cannot help you grow into being your own person, because they do not want you to. When partners practice rape consistently, they prevent you from growing into a responsive, loving sex partner of the sort you could be with a loving partner.

• The incestuous relationship causes you shame. You don't want anyone to know what you are doing. As a result, you are constantly comparing yourself with people who have appropriate relationships. You are constantly preventing yourself from opening up to friends. You are constantly acting phony, as though everything in your life is fine, when it is not. These behaviors are very hard on you, and very painful to endure.

The important thing to know is that you can have a different kind of life, that starting over is possible. You just have to give yourself permission to do so.

If you have a therapist, let her help you with the mechanics of breaking up and getting away. With the therapist, you can talk about the best ways to end the situation you're in. You'll realize that you already know how to do it and that you can do it. Most importantly, you'll realize that you want to change your situation. That's when you'll be able to make the change.

If you don't have a therapist, you can still break up and get away if you really want to. It's a good idea to: 1) Detail your reasons for wanting to get out (to provide motivation); 2) make a detailed plan —including a timeline—for getting out of the situation; 3) stick to your plan, taking it one step at a time; 4) be very careful not to tip off the abuser (by, for instance, leaving a written copy of your plan lying around the house or on a shared computer); 5) call your local rape crisis center or battered women's shelter—they can be a huge help in such situations.

16

Multiple Personalities

Childhood incest and other kinds of sexual trauma at any age can cause a survivor to form another personality. Yes, I mean a separate personality with its own feelings, name, history, knowledge and even age. In extreme cases, a personality can actually be fluent in another language or be able to play the piano, while you cannot do these things. A personality can say and do things you'd never do, and have a vocabulary more learned or less educated than yours.

You may have more than one other personality and not know about any of them. You may have other personalities that depend on you, regard you as a host, and share your consciousness. You may have personalities that get along or don't get along, that are so separate that they never communicate or are always talking to one another like members of a close-knit family.

CLAIRE

One of my clients, Claire, has four other personalities, whose ages seem to conform to the ages at which her sexual traumas occurred. These personalities all know and enjoy one another. They have their disagreements, their spats, their jealousies—all are jealous of Claire, the main personality, because she gets to talk to other people and go out into the world. The only other people the "inside people," as Claire calls them, get to talk to regularly besides Claire are me and one of Claire's friends.

But they also "do things together," as Claire puts it, such as write, draw, do artwork, and ride Claire's bicycle. They also attend a therapy group in which they get to "come out."

Three of Claire's "inside people" are female and one is a young man in his early twenties. The oldest female is in her late twenties, one is ten, and the youngest is four. The four year old seldom comes out, but the ten year old is very verbal, curious, and interested in talking to people outside.

Sometimes these personalities want to do things that are counter-productive to Claire, like drawing and dancing around the room when Claire has to study for a class. But they always respond to Claire's kind but firm orders to postpone the pleasure to a more appropriate time.

"Where do they go when they can't express themselves?" I once asked Claire.

"I don't know, really," Claire said. "They are just there, I think, maybe asleep or just watching what I do. They know what's going on with me but they can't intrude on me." Sometimes, Claire added, they do intrude, meaning they "come out" when they know they are not supposed to. "But, they always go right back when I tell them to. They don't ever disobey me. But I don't know how I'd feel if I didn't know what my personalities were doing. That must be awful!" Claire has said often, a bit jokingly but also with some real anxiety, "What if I'm an 'other' personality? What if there's a main personality in my body I don't know about?"

Will Claire's personalities ever integrate into one main personality? I don't know, and Claire is not especially eager for this integration to happen. She enjoys her relationships with her "inside people" too much to think of parting with them right now. They protected her from real trauma when it occurred, and she feels they now deserve some fun and kind treatment.

Talking with Claire's personalities is like talking with people who are actually different from Claire. The male has a deeper voice and talks like a male with the interests of a male. The ten year old has the interests and syntax of a ten year old. The four year old is wide-eyed, very curious, and also quite shy. It's painful to think that terrible rapes caused these personalities to come into existence.

Interestingly, Claire is acting like a good mother to her personalities. That's probably because her own mother never protected her from the kinds of bullying from other children that led to Claire's childhood sexual assaults. Even though she never had an effective, protective mother she could trust, Claire is protective and loving of her own personalities.

But then, Claire is learning to be a good mother to herself. "My personalities are really just parts of me," she has said many times. "They are the parts of me that got separated from me when I got hurt."

Multiples' problems

People with multiple personality disorder, or as it's now called, dissociative identity disorder (DID), do not have an easy life. One problem they face is the reaction of other people. Unfortunately, others aren't as charmed by people with DID as I have learned to be. They are often horrified, disgusted, frightened, and repulsed by the idea that personalities are shifting within the same body—or they consider the very concept of multiple personalities ridiculous. Claire tried attending a therapy group for survivors of sexual assault, thinking that her other personalities would be welcome. This was not the case. When Claire announced to the group that she had "others" and they wanted to come out and talk to the group directly, she got a cold reception. The group leaders and other group members felt "creeped out," as one put it. Claire was devastated by this response and so were her "others." It took several weeks of therapy to deal with her feelings of rejection and her sense of being a "freaking freak," as she put it.

Fortunately, Claire found a more accepting therapy group she now attends. And she was able to use the feelings triggered in her by the first group to retrieve long-repressed childhood memories of being rejected and ostracized by her siblings, her parents, and the other kids in her rural neighborhood. She was also able to come to terms with a life-long belief that she was inherently "bad, just by living," and to see that that wasn't true.

Another problem multiples struggle with is dissonance among the personalities. The personalities are often at odds, much like family members who cannot get along. They struggle for power, attention, and self-expression, just like people do in actual families. A therapist I know said that treating such multiples and their personalities is just like doing family therapy.

140 PRESENT AND FUTURE

Do you have other personalities?

I'm not trying to scare you, just alert you to the possibility that you might have DID. (And it is just that: a possibility. Simply because you were abused does not automatically mean your personality is split.) Here are some of the symptoms that might mean you're suffering from DID:

• Separate sets of clothes, lifestyles, beliefs. When you're in one lifestyle, you can't relate to the other at all.

• Talking to yourself and getting answers you don't create —answers that seem to come from someone else.

• Having people tell you that you were seen somewhere and not being able to remember going there.

• Not knowing how you accomplish tasks. You'll see you've written a great paper for a school assignment, for instance, but not know how you did it. (A friend who had multiple personalities had a genius "other" who could whip out a perfect, well-researched, 20-page academic paper in a day. The problem was, this friend often had to present these papers to the class or at conferences without really knowing what the paper was about. Why didn't the "genius" personality do the presentation? My friend never knew, because that personality would not say. But the teachers were always surprised when such a brilliant writer gave such a bumbling presentation.)

• You keep things in your house you don't use or even like. (This same friend kept children's toys in a basket in her closet. For years, she had no idea why the toys were there or why she occasionally bought new toys for the basket. In therapy, she finally found out that one of her personalities was a nine-year-old boy who came out at night and played with the toys.)

• You talk to people in what you think is a normal way and they look at you strangely. ("You seem like a different person today," they might say. Or, "You aren't the same person now," or "You really changed since I saw you last." Or something similar that indicates that you are not quite the same person they dealt with in the past.)

• You have separate social lives. (Really separate. Say, for example, you have your work friends during the day who talk about politics and history, and at night you have your upscale cocktail lounge friends, who talk of real estate deals and shopping. For instance, one client has separate lives that are so incompatible that she is in a constant state of turmoil. One life is that of a philosophy grad student in a very competitive graduate school; the other is that of an auxiliary policewoman who rides with the police at night. She dates men from her police life who care nothing for philosophy, and dates philosophy majors who can in no way relate to her police life. She is always confused about the intrusion of one of her lives into her other life. She will wonder, amazed, for instance, why a policeman she is dating would want her to change her plans to go to an academic conference so she could go to a cookout with him. And she'll wonder, equally amazed, why a professor would expect her to attend a seminar if she were needed to fill in for someone else in the auxiliary police. This client cannot seem to see that people in her separate lives have no interest in one another at all.)

• You are different people at different times of the day. (Another client is energetic, interested, and positive from the time she wakes up till about 2 pm. Around that time, another person seems to take over her body. The afternoon person is unable to deal with the same problems the client handled so well in the morning, is unable to make life work well, responds with panic to stressful incidents, and just wants to eat sweets until she gets so tired she falls asleep. The morning person, on the other hand, is not interested in eating. Sometimes, this client says, the morning person will stay most of the day if she is not fed the kind of refined carbs and sweets the afternoon person craves. But, as though lying in wait, the afternoon person will eventually come out in the late afternoon or evening, making the client want only to cancel any evening plans she might have, and instead go home and eat herself into a coma in front of the TV. "And while she's eating," this client says of her afternoon self, "this person makes food stains all over my good work clothes!" This pattern is so entrenched in this client's life that she plans for it. The client tries not to make any decisions, phone calls, or do even simple tasks in the afternoon and evening, because she is afraid they'll go badly. She also says she has to do all reading, writing, and researching in the morning, because [her exact words] "The person I become after about 2 pm doesn't want to do those things.")

What to do if you suspect you have multiple personalities

Find a psychotherapist, please. As you can see from these examples, DID can play havoc with your life. You can feel in control some of the time, but not at other times. You can have selves that are happily accomplishing one part of your life's goals, and others that have no use for those goals. You can have one life that is very demanding and satisfying, but in which you don't succeed because of the time and energy you're investing in a separate life.

Be aware: a therapist might not cure your disorder, but she will help you understand and manage it. And with understanding and management, this problem often begins to resolve itself. The main personality begins to integrate the less relevant personalities. The selves that don't fit in well atrophy and fade away.

Meanwhile, realize that there are many kinds of multiple personality conditions. They can range from slightly different selves to 300 distinctly different personalities or more, none of whom knows about the others.

Observe your symptoms with interest but detachment. That way you'll get a better understanding of what's going on. And don't feel weird. This condition is probably more common than we realize. And don't panic. Learn to deal with the different people in you as you would friends, children, or any other people you were in charge of. Learn which one is best at what and schedule your life accordingly.

How separate personalities are formed

You're probably wondering by now how this condition comes to be. The truth is, no one knows for sure. But most authorities in the psychotherapy field believe it's the result of unresolved childhood trauma. In order to bear the extreme stress and physical pain that accompany early childhood sexual assault, the child "leaves" her body. Her mind simply detaches and goes elsewhere. A separate personality can then form to deal with the pain, fear, disgust, and confusion caused by a childhood rape or other traumatic assault. That personality usually stays the age the child was when the trauma happened. Thus, suffering multiple traumas could give rise to multiple personalities. The worse the trauma, so the reasoning goes, the more separated the personality.

Some final thoughts

• Be interested in others' perceptions of you. Listen to their input about your strange behaviors. Look at their expressions when they describe how you were different yesterday.

• Search the web. Just write "multiple personality disorders" or "dissociative identity disorder" in a search engine and explore.

• Read, read, read, because there is a lot of literature on this subject. Ask your librarian for help.

17

Acting Out

Many sexual assault survivors act out their feelings—their rage, their desire for revenge, their need "to make other people hurt like I was hurt," as one client put it. This type of acting out is not planned; it's impulsive. The survivor is sorry she did it, but can't stop herself when the impulse hits. Sometimes the person hurt is the client herself.

One common, self-destructive form of acting out is taking drugs— usually crack cocaine and/or methamphetamine—or drinking alcohol, even though the survivor has been clean and sober for some time. I have at least six clients who have acted out in this way when the stress became too much for them to bear. And then, because the relief from the drugs or alcohol is so great, they continued using drugs and/or alcohol on a regular basis. All these clients think they can stop using drugs/alcohol on their own, but none has done so yet.

Allow me to tell you the obvious: Drug/alcohol use can become a problem in itself. The clients think that they need drugs/alcohol because of their sexual assault issues. But that's not the case. The truth is that they are delaying dealing with their underlying issues through their self-medication—and giving themselves additional problems in the process.

If you're abusing drugs or alcohol, you need to stop now. Many people manage to do it on their own—if they really want to. (A good self-help book can often be of real use with drug and alcohol problems. See Appendix B for some recommendations.) Others stop with the help of free recovery programs, such as SMART Recovery (based on rational emotive behavior therapy, and using scientifically based methods). Some also stop via 12-step programs such as AA and NA (which are also free), although 12-step programs are not as effective as commonly believed.

Finally, if you're physically dependent on drugs or alcohol (that is, if you suffer physical withdrawal symptoms when you stop), check yourself into a detox center. Now.

Cutting one's own flesh

I have had five clients who cut themselves before coming to me, and all stopped the cutting after our therapy began. These "cutting"(self-mutilation) clients had never explored their real feelings in previous counseling sessions, and doing so seemed to mitigate their need to cut their bodies and in other ways inflict self-pain.

Authorities in this field say cutting one's own flesh (usually with a razor blade) is a way of relieving anger, emotional stress, and emotional pressure, and that cutters almost invariably suffered severe sexual, and often physical and emotional, abuse as children. I believe that. Clients who cut themselves have told me that cutting produces a pain that is actually a strange type of pleasure. It serves as a pressure relief valve, temporarily releasing emotional discomfort, and producing a euphoria of its own.

If you cut yourself, should you stop? Yes. Absolutely. Cutting is addictive. Cutting causes scars and sometimes infection, and is disfiguring. (Do you really want to go through life always having to wear clothing to cover your arms and legs, because you're ashamed of their scars?)

The good news is that cutting is treatable. Evidence indicates that psychotherapy can help, as can certain types of drugs: opiate-blockers, such as Naltrexone, and anti-depressants, such as Prozac and Paxil.

As well, cutting is often symptomatic of severe problems such as anorexia, bipolar disorder, and borderline personality disorder. If you're cutting yourself, even occasionally, you need professional help. Now.

Destroying one's own and others' property

Property damage comes in many forms. What all have in common is that they are usually induced by rage.

I have a client who sweeps objects—including all the food, china, and cutlery for a meal—off tables and shelves when she feels rage at what her multiple perpetrators did. She doesn't care where she is, at her home or someone else's. She has been barred from her relatives' homes as a result of this behavior, and now worries that she'll act out in this way at the home of her only remaining friend. She has always helped clean up the mess in others' homes, but often leaves it lying for days in her own. "That's to remind me of what I did," she says every time.

This client is joining a group for anger management and has started taking a psychiatric medication. The group and the meds will, I hope, soon help her to stop acting out in such a destructive way. This client benefits greatly from therapy—until a rage attack hits, which can be triggered any time she is reminded of someone from her past, or when someone says something to her that triggers her memories of her rape. Could she exercise more will power when these urges come over her? Probably, but that requires effort and practice. I have taught her the cognitive-behavioral therapy (CBT) technique of changing her thoughts when she enrages herself. (In other words, to substitute more rational thoughts [that is, thoughts that serve her better] for the self-enraging thoughts induced by the "trigger.") So far she has been able to use that technique successfully only a few times. With further effort and practice, she'll probably become better at using it. And her new meds and her participation in the anger management group will probably help, too.

Stealing and embezzling

DRANGEA

Drangea is a lovely, gracious woman in her late thirties. She has three teenage children and a husband who has always been the caregiver in the home, while Drangea has always been the breadwinner. Unfortunately, her need to act out on her job might cause her to go to prison for several years.

Drangea's father was away most of the time that she was growing up. He worked as a traveling salesman and her mother worked full time in a factory, mostly from 11 am to 9 pm. Drangea's older brother Rob almost entirely raised her, her two younger brothers, and her sister. Drangea recalls that Rob "taught us everything we knew. People don't realize what a big part of childrearing teaching is." Drangea knows because of the price Rob made her pay for the lessons: "When he taught me anything, how to braid my hair, fry an egg, make my arithmetic homework right, put on my socks, drive a car, he had to put his hand down my shorts or under my dress and down my panties and rub me. I had to let him do that if I wanted to learn how to do anything!"

Rob never actually penetrated her. "I guess he was satisfied with just rubbing me up. Then he'd run away to his room and slam the door behind him and I guess masturbate. We weren't allowed to bother him during those times."

Drangea married a much older man at the age of 16, "mostly to get out of the house," and soon had three children of her own. When this man proved to be emotionally abusive and unwilling to hold a job, he said Drangea could work and he'd watch the children. "So I took these awful jobs I hated, factory jobs like my mother had, convenience store clerk jobs that were mostly graveyard shift, telephone sales jobs that were just plain ripping people off." This forced-work situation triggered Drangea's PTSD symptoms. "My husband wasn't that bad a housekeeper. But I was scared to death he was doing to my kids the sort of things my brother did to me—I'd just start worrying about it at work and not be able to get it out of my mind. I'd want to just run home and make sure he was leaving them alone. I knew it was irrational, but I couldn't stop the fear. Then I started having flashbacks of my brother feeling me up when a boss tried to teach me anything new. It was so bad."

Then a wealthy, elderly couple offered Drangea a job as their caretaker when they could no longer run their own household. "I had complete charge of all their financial transactions, complete access to all their bank accounts. I wrote the checks to pay all their bills."

Soon, Drangea found herself "self-medicating" by writing checks to herself. "If my employers kept me late for some reason, or insisted on talking about their great grandchildren but not letting me talk about my kids, I'd write a check to myself. I'd just get even with them by writing myself a nice check." The amount of the check depended on how strongly Drangea felt at the time. "They'd had a happy life, their children had happy lives and accomplished lots of things, so had their grandchildren, and now their great grandchildren were just wonderful too. I'd pretend to ooh and aah over those kids when they came to visit, but inside I'd be seething with so much jealousy I could hardly stay sane. It wasn't fair all these people had so much when I never did. So I'd slip away to my little office, get the checkbook and write myself a nice check." Drangea never spent the money on herself; she just deposited it in her family's account, telling her husband the elderly couple had given her the money as a "sort of bonus. Of course, he believed me. The problem was, he got used to having that money and got dependent on it for clothes and food for the kids." When Drangea tried to stop her embezzling, her husband became angry with her. "I was pressured by my own guilt to stop, and then by his demands to keep getting that money and ask for more."

Drangea said she was almost relieved when her employers' accountant recognized her embezzlement and brought it to her employers' attention. "I was so embarrassed, I wanted to die. But I was also so glad that something had stopped me because I knew I could never have done it myself."

As of this writing, Drangea is facing a maximum prison sentence of 20 years. She is terrified of being incarcerated, but believes she deserves every punishment she gets.

But does she deserve to be incarcerated? I don't think so. I think she needs a plan of restitution (the total of her embezzlement came to about $14,000, a sum she could easily repay), and a sentence of at least a year of intense therapy. She needs the therapy to deal with the feelings from her childhood and teenage sexual molestation. Like most survivors, she married someone who would also exploit her, and so never had a chance to develop a fully functioning conscience or a sense of right and wrong.

If there were a moral system operating in the world, Drangea thought, she was forced to live outside of it. That meant she could take from others in much the same way others had taken from her. Fortunately, she had enough of a conscience to feel guilty about what she did to her employers—she only enjoyed the moment of revenge she experienced when she wrote the checks; later, she felt remorse.

It's clear that Drangea's thefts were a reaction against her brother's theft of sexual favors from Drangea. This "taking," Drangea learned in childhood, was how one dealt with strong impulses of any kind. Drangea, in my opinion, never had a chance. She is as much a victim as her employers and deserves to be treated as such.

LISSY

Lissy's brother abused her from the time she was five until she was 13. Her family, instead of getting her into treatment, told her she was lying and exiled her from the family—or so she says. It's hard to believe Lissy because she says she began using methamphetamine at the age of 13, is still apparently using it, and heavy meth use plays havoc with the memory and makes lying as natural as truth telling.

Today, Lissy is a ravaged-looking woman of 35 whose off-and-on use of meth for the past 20 years has made her a walking skeleton with bulging eyes and bad teeth. It's a testament to the need for certified nursing assistants that she is able to work in nursing homes despite her appearance and her speech, which is so rapid it is sometimes impossible to understand.

The part of Lissy's story I believe is that she "just ha[s] to take" pretty bottles the nursing home residents leave out on their nightstands and bureaus. "I don't do anything with these bottles," Lissy says. "I just line them up at my house and look at them. I need to tell you I do this and I don't know why I do it." If these "pretty bottles" could be sold for drugs, I would have guessed immediately why Lissy stole them. But they have no resale value at all, and their loss makes the nursing home residents very sad. "It's like the more family value the bottle has, say if I know it was a gift from a daughter or sister or someone who loves this old lady, I just have to steal it all the more. I even try to stop myself from doing it, but I can never resist."

If Lissy were able to stop her drug taking and become what we call "therapy ready," she might be able to connect her thefts to her need to get her family to love her, to give to her, instead of to her perpetrator. She might see that her patients are never going to love her as her family should have. But she doesn't see this, and so she displaces her anger onto the nursing home residents, stealing from them the symbols of love from their families.

Verbal harassment

A few of my clients resort to "telephonitis" when they act out. They call their perpetrators, or family members they think are not treating them well, dozens of times in an hour. They call friends they feel insulted them and threaten to get these people fired from their jobs, evicted from their apartments, and to turn their friends and relatives against them.

These verbal attacks are irrational, but briefly satisfying to the survivor who is driven to perform them. Instead of suffering her own anxiety and rage, the survivor inflicts anxiety and rage upon others—a strategy that brings the survivor immediate relief. But the medium- and long-term results are always bad. They often involve restraining orders against the survivor. And eventually this type of verbal harassment isolates the survivor from everyone she could have once counted on for support.

But, alas, the survivor seldom feels sorry for what she did. As one of these "telephoners" said to me recently, "These people should know I don't mean it when I say these things, that I'm just getting things off my chest. I don't know why they take it so hard." And once again, the survivor gets to feel like a victim, a role she has come to feel comfortable in, even if she doesn't like it very much.

If you find the telephone to be your acting-out weapon of choice, find hot lines and maybe one relative you can talk to as needed on a 24/7 basis. If you can reach anyone to help you with your rage attacks, you'll lose your need to inflict pain and fear on others. And you'll stop driving away people who love you.

18

When the Victim Becomes a Perpetrator

In their book, *Treating the Adult Survivor of Childhood Sexual Abuse*, the authors, Jody Messler Davies and Mary Gail Frawley, talk about a girl from a wealthy family whose very successful father had sex with her when she was a child. The abuse stopped when the girl went off to boarding school. However, she would go into town on weekends and frequent local "townie" bars, where she would find older men and have sex with them. This pattern continued into her adult life. Even though she was very successful in her career, this survivor went on seeking older, lower socioeconomic class sex partners in rough, downscale bars.

Perhaps some of these men were smitten with the young, beautiful, upper-class woman seducing them. Perhaps some of these men felt that they had been given a wonderful, unexpected lease on life, believing that this girl appreciated special qualities in them. And perhaps these same men felt betrayed and abandoned when the sex was never offered to them again. Because of these behaviors, we can imagine this survivor as a perpetrator—sexually using her victims in ways that mimic desire.

Children undergoing abuse who act out their sexual abuse on other children (which is likely to happen if they aren't treated) vividly illustrate the sad truth that survivors often act out by becoming sexual predators themselves.

The truth is, rape and sexual abuse can make you need sex—callous, cruel, unfeeling sex—as much as you hate touching and affection, especially from people who care. When you find yourself seeking that kind of sex and putting off loving sex, please, get help. Soon.

Meanwhile, here are some ideas for avoiding the dangers of acting out: Resist urges to roam the bars at night or on your lunch hour, seeking stranger sex. Resist the need to have sex on a first date, or with a friend's husband, or someone else who is inappropriate. Resist the urge to seduce a grown child's friend or, in fact, the grown child her or himself. You don't have to be ashamed of these desires, but you do have to resist acting on them.

Resist the urge to withhold sex from someone who has the right to expect it from you. Try as hard as you can to accept the sexual overtures of a partner you love and who loves you. You can do it. But it won't, alas, be easy.

Learning to tolerate loving sex again can be a matter of will power. You might have to put up with it in small doses until you get used to it again and can allow yourself to enjoy it. You might need years of willpower-driven sexual contact before you can enjoy erotic play with someone who loves you, but meanwhile you'll be keeping your partner happy, and that's important, indeed. Your partner loves and supports you, but you can't expect him or her to be celibate forever. That's just not fair.

I have many clients who expect me to take their side against partners who want sexual intimacy again before they're ready. I have to tell them I can't take sides, that they might never be ready, and so they'll have to work at having loving sex again.

Perpetrator tendencies

• **Interest in becoming a prostitute**. You might actually find yourself thinking that you could do that job, about what kind of clothes you'd wear, and how you would solicit customers.

• **Interest in seducing the innocent**, like children. No, you're not a perverted person. You just have a need, which is totally natural and to be expected, to re-enact your sexual violence. Part of that need might be a desire for victims who (as you were) would be most damaged by sexual assault.

• **Need to stalk**. I have seen this symptom again and again in my clients. One, a victim of rape by three college athletes who had offered her a ride home after a party, actually got arrested for stalking. Her primary victim? Her psychologist. "I wanted her to know what it was like, having her life violated," this woman said. She showed up again and again on the psychologist's front porch, in her garage, and sitting on her car at the end of the day.

The more this client stalked, the more she needed to stalk. Restraining orders had absolutely no effect on this woman. During the five years this client spent in prison for violating restraining orders, she wrote to the psychologist every day, and tried calling her with the few phone calls she was allowed. This client was later mine, and here is how she explained—in despair—her behavior: "I just wanted her to understand why I was doing all that. I guess I was stalking her in a secondary way so I could make her understand why I had to stalk her in the first place."

That client never did understand that stalking is inappropriate, let alone morally wrong. She stopped being what we call "therapy ready" when a change in her psychiatric medications caused her to fall apart, mentally and emotionally. I have always wondered if this client began stalking her psychologist because of her psychosis or if the psychotic symptoms were brought on by her acting out her need to stalk. I suspect her need to stalk began as a normal PTSD symptom that triggered her psychosis when she acted upon it. Stalking became addictive for this client, overcoming the last bit of reasoning ability she had left.

Other clients have stalked people—perpetrators, people they suspected of being perpetrators, and anyone else who might be a wrongdoer—when they could have gotten the information they wanted by making phone calls or looking on the Internet. One client stalked the boyfriend of her perpetrator (a gay man who was also a rapist of women) night after night after work, trying to find out where the perpetrator lived. She would drive to the place where the boyfriend worked, then try to follow him home. When she finally tracked him to a large apartment complex, she stalked him on foot to see what apartment he went to. When told she could have gotten this information from the police, because her perpetrator was then in jail, this client looked dazed. "Oh," she said, "I'd never do that. The police address might be wrong." This client's new boyfriend finally persuaded her to stop stalking, because he was afraid she'd get in an accident or be arrested for stalking, or worse, get hurt if the perp found out what she was doing.

• **Need to punish**. Rape victims find themselves wanting to punish people they love, such as family members, people who want to help them, such as therapists and physicians, and people who haven't been raped, such as co-workers or anyone else. (In my case, this punishment by rape victims takes the form of no-shows [not showing up to an appointment or calling to cancel], making appointments and then routinely canceling, etc.)

One such client inflicted punishment by going to her boyfriend's place of business when she was upset with him for any reason, and accusing his boss of having an affair with him. Everyone in the boyfriend's office found these visits entertaining for awhile, and told the boyfriend he was lucky to have such a spitfire for a girlfriend. Even the boss—who was an understanding woman—tolerated these visits. But eventually she got tired of them and told the client's boyfriend that if the girlfriend showed up in a blazing temper one more time, she would have to let him go. Sadly, my client did show up one more time, despite the boyfriend's warning about the consequences, resulting in his being fired. That did not stop my client's visits to the ex-boss —or to the now ex-boyfriend. She violated restraining orders served by both of her stalking victims and is now facing jail time. Why, you ask, could she not stop her stalking activities? Because the release of tension they provided was stronger than any fear of consequences. This client was seduced at the age of six by an uncle whom she adored, and was then abandoned by him at the age of ten, when he married a beautiful woman the client hates to this day for "taking him away from me."

Another client has her boyfriend act out for her. She comes to therapy full of complaints about her boyfriend's stalking activities— how he shows up on her doorstep when she comes home, how he calls her all night to see where she's been and who she's with, and follows her car now and then to see where she's going. When this client did not break up with this boyfriend despite her fear of him, I began to suspect that she wanted him to stalk her. When the boyfriend broke up with her briefly because he became attracted to someone else, she subjected him to the same kind of stalking he had inflicted on her. "I can't stop calling him!" the client said. "And I drove by his house four times last week! I don't understand myself at all." She is now working on the feelings aroused in her by seeing her perpetrator, a handsome brother-in-law who abused her sexually from the age of five to fourteen, at church or on visits to her parents' home with his beautiful wife– the client's own older sister. This client realizes now that she wanted him to desire her during those times and is secretly happy when her boyfriend acts out this desire in real life. When she thought that her boyfriend was interested in someone else, this client found herself acting out her rage at her brother-in-law by becoming a stalker herself.

The need to punish is so much a form of acting out old rage at perpetrators, people who didn't stop the perpetrators, and people adored by the perpetrators, that it could be called pure theatre. It provides the same instant cathartic release as a play or film. But it's dangerous because it can become addictive and can escalate. It's also dangerous because it can take very ugly, destructive forms. This ugliness is often so insidious that it goes unnoticed by anyone but the victim of the punishment. Some survivors target certain people, especially helpless people such as children, as punishment receivers and force them to withstand all kinds of bad treatment. While, I am glad to say, I have not had clients who acted out such urges, I have had a few who recognized these urges in themselves. These clients do not want to be near children at all—which is sad because they know they can never be parents.

Here's what I want you to take away from this chapter: All of these forms of perpetrating feel good. Sometimes, they feel very good. You are not to be blamed because you have urges to punish, stalk, or even perpetrate in various ways. But in the long run these behaviors would hurt not only those you victimize, but you as well. That's why you have to be extremely aware of your impulses to become a perpetrator yourself, and to nip them in the bud.

19

Guilty Pleasures:
When Something Bad Feels Good

Most sexual assault agencies have a department that sends people—usually volunteers—to the emergency room to be with rape victims while they are getting medical care and providing forensic evidence. These volunteers also visit the victims if the victims are hospitalized. I took the 40-hour training required to become one of these volunteers, but found I was not suited to this type of crisis work. I just wasn't tough enough.

But I was fascinated—and, yes, horrified—by a story one of the training instructors told me. She had been visiting a seven-year-old girl who was hospitalized because she had been sexually assaulted by her father and injured physically in the process. Suddenly, the little girl asked the instructor to please turn her head. "I have to do something nasty now," the child explained. When the instructor turned her head away, she could still see the child well enough to know that the child was masturbating. What did the instructor do? "I told her the masturbation was all right to do, but had to be continued in the restroom."

The truth is, most survivors begin liking, then needing, the kind of sex they get from their perpetrators. Children are especially vulnerable to sex addiction because their perpetrators tend to groom them carefully. (And, yes, let me stress this fact again: even small children are capable of sexual response.) The perpetrators train and coach children to behave sexually just like adults. The child's need for attention, affection, and understanding becomes mixed up with her prematurely awakened need for sex.

But deep down, children know, despite the perp's assurances that it is a good thing, what is happening is not good. Yet they know it feels good. This seems to lead them to need sex with people who treat them badly. It takes therapy—often a great deal of therapy—to help them want, enjoy, and be aroused by men or women who treat them well.

Some survivors cannot remember the abusive sex feeling good. They tell me they hated every minute of it. But these survivors tend to suffer what we call "somatic" symptoms for the rest of their lives. Somatic symptoms are emotionally caused physical symptoms. These symptoms can apparently be triggered by injuries incurred many years after the sexual abuse—injuries that may seem mild but throw the survivor into absolute misery. One of my clients has been in and out of hospitals for over 20 years for unexplained pains in her abdomen. She began having these pains one day after lifting a box on her job. Extensive tests revealed nothing amiss at the time and continue to show nothing now. Yet the pain is so bad she can sometimes hardly walk.

I think that the pain this client suffers is her way of blocking pleasurable memories. She is not only unwilling to admit that she could have enjoyed the sexual abuse she was subjected to from age four to seven by her uncle, but she becomes enraged at the thought of it. Yet her abuse occurred annually, on summer visits to this uncle's house—visits she agreed to. This client told me that she had to go on these visits because she had no choice; she just couldn't get out of them. This explanation does not hold water. Her parents and other relatives appear to have been very loving to her at the time. They became enraged when they finally heard about the abuse, and stopped the visits immediately. Had the uncle not died of a heart attack soon after, he would probably have been charged and imprisoned.

It seems likely that the abuse was physically pleasurable for this client in ways she still cannot face. She was very fond of her uncle's wife, who treated her as a beloved niece. From her comments in therapy, it also seems likely that this client hates herself deeply for being a willing partner in the sexual betrayal of her aunt.

Today, this client can only enjoy sex with men who are immature, possessive, and prone to temper tantrums. Her current boyfriend sulks every time he thinks she is friendly with another man. He accuses her of flirting with her car mechanic, for instance, yet refuses to do any work on her car himself, even though he used to be a mechanic.

This client's uncle told her while he was abusing her that he wanted her all for himself and that she must never tell anyone about their special time together. I think she now conflates this kind of obsessive possessiveness with sexual pleasure. If she could acknowledge the pleasure she felt while she was being sexually abused as a child, and process the feelings of betraying her aunt, she might experience relief from her symptoms. I can't say for sure, but I have a strong feeling that this would be so. But she still denies the possibility that she experienced pleasure from her abuse.

The truth is, her uncle probably groomed her to be a sexual partner, and such abusers always provide pleasure to the victims in subtle, addictive ways.

Few perpetrators want their quarry to feel like a victim who is forced into having sex. They want the child to behave like a little lover cooperating out of sexual desire and need. To this end, perpetrators often groom little girls and boys much in the manner a dog groomer carefully and patiently grooms a special dog for performing in a show. Like the dog groomer, the perp grooms the child by first making her enjoy the process, and then grooms her again for performing well. This grooming is often so successful that the victim will actually get excited thinking about or anticipating the molestation.

Grooming explained

Even after hearing hundreds of victims' stories, I still found it hard to write this section. Some of the following may seem prurient to you, and you may wonder why I have to go into such detail. It's because I have seen first hand that failure to look at details has enabled my clients to continue being in denial. This means they are not able to talk about their feelings in a way that will relieve their extreme guilt and expedite their recovery—their actual recovery, and not a false recovery that keeps them re-enacting their abuse over and over with new partners all their lives.

Grooming usually begins with kind and gentle attention, and stroking of some sort. The perp's hand will linger on an arm or back or thigh at first, then progress from these areas to the side of the breast, the inside of the thigh, the tummy. Next, the groomer will begin rubbing these areas gently and go underneath the clothes to the bare skin. Sometimes the perp will say, "You're so pretty, you smell so good," and "Does this feel good? I want you to feel good," and the like.

Sooner or later, sometimes in the initial abuse session, sometimes over a period of days or weeks, the fondling progresses to the genital area. Digital insertion begins. The perp teaches the victim how to fondle his genitals. Then he teaches the victim how to perform—and enjoy—mutual oral stimulation. One client remembers how her abuse began with back scratching from her father when she was 11 years old. "I would sit on his lap and he would scratch in the middle for awhile, then move his hand ever more toward my breast. I'd get so aroused I'd tell him, 'That feels good.'" This behavior went on for about four months, progressing slowly but surely to breast and nipple fondling. Then one day, the client's mother came home, realized what was going on and put a stop to it immediately. She pulled the client off her father's lap and told her to leave the room. "I could hear her yelling at him from outside the door," the client said. "I didn't know what to think at the time." After this incident, the client missed the fondling terribly: "I'd beg my father to let me sit on his lap when my mother wasn't home. I'd tell him I needed 'so bad' to have my back scratched, but he always said 'no.' He never really liked me after that." Indeed, that marked the beginning of the client's downward spiral. "I was just always feeling so ashamed. And my father made me ashamed of myself," the client said. "I started wearing lipstick then, and he always called me a slut when I put makeup on. I can't count the number of times he said, 'You look like a whore,' when he saw me with lipstick. My mother always agreed with him and the two of them would stand there together, calling me a whore and saying I looked awful."

As so often happens after such incidents, the back scratching was never mentioned in the client's childhood home again. The client tried denying it happened in therapy, and, when that didn't work, denied that it was a big deal.

But finally, after almost a year of therapy, she was willing to acknowledge it was no accident that she kept getting involved in triangle relationships. She admitted that these affairs always began with her seducing men who had wives or girlfriends. She would initiate these flings by "coming on to the men sexually in their cars or whenever I was alone with them for any length of time." Usually, she said, the men reciprocated—but they seldom stayed in the affair for long. "They'd always feel so ashamed of what they were doing with me. And I'd feel so scared they'd leave because I loved the fondling so much. I put up with the intercourse, which the men always insisted on, but it was the fondling I really, really loved."

Today, this client is still processing her part in her sexual abuse. She thinks it's finally possible to do this work because both of her parents have been dead for several years. "While they were alive, I couldn't even let myself remember that fondling period. But it was always there in the back of my mind, like this sense that I was a bad seed who tried to seduce my father and didn't care if it hurt my mother." The client is now realizing that she never felt wanted by her parents, that her mother was jealous of her from the time she was born, and that her father was jealous of her because of the time her mother spent on her. She now understands that she felt she ruined her parents' lives from the time she was born. "They had only been married nine months," she told me. "They were in no way ready to have a baby." She believes, as do I, that she would never have wanted sexual contact with her father had she gotten the nonsexual affection and affirmation she needed from him to feel pretty and secure.

Boys are groomed via companionship from older males who eroticize the friendship and educate their prey about sex between males. Sometimes another boy is involved who is near or at the same age as the predator, and sometimes the abuse takes place in threesomes. In these cases, survivors have told me, the pleasure is increased exponentially.

One such client said he was groomed for this kind of activity by the husband of the woman who employed his mother as a housecleaner. His mom would take the client along on the job because he was too young—eleven years old at the time—to be left alone. The husband, who was retired, would invite this boy to watch football with him in the den while the "women did their cleaning." The first two times, the man was very kind and caring to the boy, often telling him how nice it was to have company because his wife didn't like sports. The third time, the man asked the boy if he wanted a sweater the man could no longer wear. Trying on the sweater required the boy to take off his shirt. "The man said I had real nice arms and a beautiful chest, that I was built like a tight end," said my client. "The next thing I knew, this man was running his hands across my shoulders, saying he wanted to see if I liked being massaged. It all felt so good, I didn't want to have him stop." The back massage soon lead to an examination of the boy's legs and abdomen and a request that the boy remove his jeans so the man could see the rest of his body. "I was like mesmerized. And so excited, I could hardly think," the boy said. Soon, the man was fondling the boy's private parts, saying softly they were beautiful. Then came oral sex from the man, producing a pleasure "I never knew existed," the boy said. The man did not wait until the following week to see the boy. He called him up at home and arranged with his mom to take the boy bowling. "We went straight to a motel and I learned how to give him the pleasure he was giving me." On their next "bowling" date, the man had with him a young boy who was 13 and "incredibly good looking, like a movie star." A three-way relationship started that night and continued for over a year. It ended when the older man died suddenly of a heart attack and the older boy died of alcohol poisoning. Today, this client is unable to sustain a relationship with a woman and lives in terror of being gay. He has quit or been fired from every job he's ever held because he always fears that some man he works with "is coming on" to him. Today, he is afraid to work anywhere and cannot support himself.

Another client, as a 12-year-old altar boy, was groomed by a priest. "This priest would take me into his office and feel me all over, ending up at my crotch. Then he'd stop. He wouldn't say a word, just get up and say he was finished with me and I could go." This boy would leave feeling so excited he could hardly stand it. "The day the priest made me take off my clothes and gave me oral sex was such a relief for me physically I never will forget it. I was ready to do anything he wanted, just to get that sexual release." Three priests molested this boy over the next five years, until his father smelled semen on him when he came home from church one day and made him tell all. Today, this client is suffering all kinds of symptoms. But his feeling of revulsion at having sex with his wife bothers him most of all.

These stories show how easily children can be aroused when the person grooming them has won their trust. Once children believe an adult likes them and has their best interests in mind, they will most likely want to please that adult—especially if their own pleasure is awakened.

So please, let yourself remember the pleasure you experienced during your sexual abuse. Don't be ashamed if it leads to being re-aroused now. It's not your fault. You felt that way—and perhaps still feel that way—because you were and still are a sexual being. You don't need to feel guilt. Everything is all right—and so are you.

And again, realize that you're not alone. Realize that others have gone through the same horrors as you and have recovered.

A FINAL WORD

This book is about your mother's role in your sexual trauma. But it's also about all the feelings relating to your abuse, impulses resulting from it, and reactions to it that you weren't expecting.

And this book is about my experiences with hundreds of clients. The sheer number of clients tires me and sometimes comes close to burning me out. But it also allows me to see patterns in survivors that other professionals might not.

You should know about others' experiences. If you do, you'll know you're not alone, not going insane, and not intrinsically bad, or, as one client put it, "damaged goods." You'll know you're not really a predator or a perpetrator yourself. And you'll know you don't have to be a victim of anyone who chooses to exploit you or of anyone who wants to hurt you.

And, most of all, you are not what your mother might like to think you are—unattractive, incompetent, a liar, or a shameless seductress who brought sexual trauma on herself. You might think you are one or more of these things, but trust me, you are not.

If you aren't able to get psychotherapy, you'll always have this book to rely on. Please use it whenever doubts, fears, flashbacks, mean impulses, disgust, and shame sneak into your mind and set up camp. Please also use the references and contacts listed in the following appendixes. And if worse comes to worst, you can relocate to Tucson and visit our Center Against Sexual Assault. The move might be worth it if it helps you reclaim your life.

In any case, I leave you with hope and my tears. I'm crying right now as I write this last sentence because I want so much for you to find the help you both need and deserve.

A

Getting Help

The types of help recommended for sexual trauma are psychotherapy, counseling, trauma treatment (such as hypnosis and eye movement desensitization reinforcement), support groups, and, sometimes, psychiatric medications. Let's start with support groups first, because these are the most common form of help. You can, if you have to, start one yourself. It only takes one other person to have a support group.

Support groups

These groups consist of people who share similar experiences. You've undoubtedly heard of 12-step groups that target people who have (or had) issues with alcohol, drugs, food, and loved ones who have these addictions. There are also groups for the recently bereaved, for parents whose children have been murdered, and for survivors of just about any kind of trauma you can name.

Here are the benefits sexual trauma survivors get from support groups: being understood; knowing they are not alone; being able to exchange information on what helps; and exchanging phone numbers with people they can call in emotional emergencies.

In 12-step groups, in contrast to the type of survivors' self-help groups I recommend, there are always steps to follow and higher powers to call upon. (All 12-step groups—from Alcoholics Anonymous to Gamblers Anonymous to Clutterers Anonymous—follow a near-identical set of "spiritual" steps centered around God and prayer.)* A

---

* There is a 12-step group called Incest Survivors Anonymous. It is not tailored to the needs of incest survivors. Its purpose, like that of all other 12-step groups, is to get attendees to follow the 12 steps.

group for survivors would not need these kinds of steps and would probably not have a rigid 12-step structure in its meetings. The purpose of survivors' groups is sharing, getting comfort, and giving comfort. These activities help the healing process progress at a faster, more consistent rate than if the survivor was isolated.

Why you may not like the idea of support groups

Many see support group meetings as self-pity sessions. "I don't want to be around people who are also suffering," one client said. Another remarks, "They're always competing to see who suffered the worst." Support groups can also seem repetitive: "I don't want to be around people who complain about the same things all the time —that's boring," yet another client said. And the stories told in these groups can be difficult to hear: "If I hear anybody talk about sexual assault, I start getting flashbacks," another client said when I suggested she join a support group.

These are valid complaints. Others' stories of their sexual assaults could retrigger your symptoms. Others' needs to repeat their stories over and over might bore you. Others' needs to have their trauma be worse than anyone else's could annoy you no end. But the camaraderie from people who understand what you went through, how your symptoms are affecting you, and how your trauma derailed your life, might outweigh the negative aspects. So, please try a support group despite your misgivings, and get the most out of it you can.

How to tell if a support group is well run

A designated facilitator should keep the group on task at every meeting. Time for speaking should be limited so that everyone who wants to can get a chance to share. There should be a check-in so that everyone can say how they're doing at the beginning of each meeting. Arguing, criticism, and/or other acting out should not be allowed.

The facilitator should regulate members' unwanted behavior and know when to ask such questions as, "Does anyone have any ideas about Jim's problem with his mother's blaming of him for being molested? Have any of you been in that situation?"

He or she should also remind members to be supportive of one another, and not critical. Therapy group members can tell one another what they really think of other members, but support group members must be supportive.

Fifteen minutes or so should normally be devoted to psycho-education. This can include sharing of articles on flashbacks, irritability and other symptoms of sexual trauma, a guest speaker who is an expert on sexual trauma, or a report on a book dealing with sexual trauma that a member has found helpful—or not helpful, as the case might be.

Eye movement desensitization reinforcement (EMDR)

Developed to help war veterans with PTSD symptoms, EMDR consists of the clinician moving two fingers back and forth while the client follows the fingers with her eyes and answers questions about her trauma. This concentration on the moving fingers is said to help the client integrate her trauma experiences, and thus become better able to deal with them. It must be done by a certified EMDR practitioner who can handle the descriptions of the client's traumas without wincing or reacting in other ways. Clients who have been through EMDR have told me that it is not a miracle cure, but that it has helped them somewhat and has enabled them to reach new levels of understanding. Studies of EMDR indicate that it can be extremely effective, and that its effects seem immediate.

Hypnosis

I cannot recommend hypnosis for people with PTSD symptoms unless the hypnotist is also a psychotherapist. Hypnotists must be able to deal with emotions, such as terror and rage, that are likely to surface while a client is in a hypnotic trance. The reason for this is that hypnosis does not always go well when violent memories are involved, and the client stands a real chance of needing to be hospitalized if terrifying memories resurface quickly, especially in the presence of someone the client doesn't know and trust.

Counseling

Counseling is a sort of coaching designed to help a client manage, repress, and "get over" her PTSD symptoms. Counseling can be helpful in the short run, especially if a client needs to be alert on her job or able to participate fully in a relationship. It is also good when the survivor needs someone to talk to, someone who is not in denial about the client's feelings (as partners and other family members often are), and is positive about her chances for recovery.

Counseling is not good when the counselor says the client should be "cured" before the client is feeling better. Or when the counselor says the counseling is at an end because, in the counselor's opinion, the client is cured. It is not good when the counselor minimizes the client's PTSD symptoms. It is not good when the counselor tells the client that the problem of the sexual assault is solved and should never come up again. It is not good when the counselor says that the client's symptoms are the result of her "dwelling" too much on the event and will clear up if she puts it out of her mind. It is not good when the counselor tells the client how the client should feel instead of asking the client what she's feeling. It is not good when the counselor is more interested in talking than listening—really paying attention—to what the client has to say.

Clients have described all these behaviors by counselors, and I've seen first hand the damage they do. That damage includes:

- loss of faith by the client in his own feelings
- fear that she is not meeting the counselor's standards
- failure to deal with other issues associated with the trauma —such as the client's feelings about her mother
- feelings of worthlessness arising from the counselor's disrespect of her feelings
- extreme anger at the counselor for this disrespect and then hatred of himself for feeling anger at someone who is trying to help him

I have seen these results time and time again. But yes, there are good counselors.

Characteristics of a good counselor

- He makes you feel understood, cared about, and safe.
- She helps you understand your symptoms.
- She helps you manage your symptoms in ways that are practical.
- He gives you exercises or other strategies to use when symptoms arise.
- She is always gentle and encouraging.

Characteristics of a bad counselor

- She makes you feel blamed, responsible in part for what happened, self-indulgent for wanting to talk about what happened, unwilling to "get over it and move on," and/or guilty.
- She makes you feel that her advice works and it's your fault if you can't benefit from it.
- He makes you feel that he's got a great reputation and helps many, many people, and if you aren't helped, then you are not a good client.
- She makes you feel bad about yourself in some way in almost every session.

If the counselor puts you in a group

Many counseling programs for sexual trauma survivors consist of group therapy as well as individual counseling. Therapy groups help members understand how they interact with people, form relationships, respond to certain behaviors in others and, especially, re-enact with other people the feelings they had in their families.

Therapy groups can be very helpful if they are carefully run by leaders who are fair, if they include only survivors of sexual trauma, and if they do not include perpetrators as well as victims.

Some counselors believe that sexual assault therapy groups should include perpetrators, because they need help as well, and their presence helps survivors see that perpetrators are human beings, too. The practice of including perpetrators might help the perpetrators, but it will almost always hurt the survivors. The survivors' symptoms are not only likely to be retriggered by the presence of perpetrators, but retriggered so badly that the survivors can be retraumatized.

Many counselors include people in their groups who are not survivors of sexual assault. That's because they fail to understand that sexual trauma is a specialized area that is seldom understood by people who have not experienced it. Here's an example of what can happen to a sexual assault survivor in a "mixed therapy" group.

A client had seen a counselor who believed that the less time spent on the client's sexual assault, the better. The counselor believed the client's escalating symptoms—crying all the time, anger outbursts, fear of any sexual activity with her husband, and constant guilt that made her suicidal—were "put on" by the client.

The counselor insisted the client join a large group that included people with all kinds of issues, from drug users to widows unable to stop grieving to single people who could not form relationships. When the client tried talking about her symptoms in this group, the other group members told her not to go into details of her assault because, as one put it, "we find the details inappropriate." They told her she was thinking too much about herself and should concentrate on the other members' problems; they also told her she should be over the assault by now, because it had been over a year since it happened. In her individual counseling sessions, the counselor told her that the other group members had valid points she should take to heart. "See?" this counselor said, "I'm not the only one who believes that you should be controlling your symptoms and becoming interested in other people besides yourself."

The client continued to deteriorate rapidly while seeing this counselor and attending the mixed group sessions. She felt suicidal for days after every group meeting, and began cutting herself after every meeting in an attempt to manage the feelings of self-hatred evoked by the other group members' comments. She relapsed into alcohol abuse, and was finally forced by family members to enter inpatient treatment to deal with her self-mutilation and suicide threats.

By the time she came to see me, she was drinking heavily, fighting constantly with her family, and thinking of abandoning them and getting out of town. "But I knew I'd just take myself with me," she said, "and that would defeat the whole purpose of running away."

The first thing I did for this client was to tell her I believed her. The second thing was to tell her I wanted to hear about her symptoms—over and over and over again if she needed to recite them over and over and over again. The third thing was to tell her she had a right to feel every feeling she felt, no matter how bad she might think the feeling was. This client has now, eight sessions later, stopped drinking alcohol, stopped cutting herself, and stopped smoking. When she has bad feelings now, she sands her wooden floors, which she says is therapeutic and gives her a sense of accomplishment. She is still fighting with her family members, but is no longer ashamed of being angry with them. She also loves being able to dwell on her assault if she needs to, for as long as she needs to. And, as a result, she needs to do that less and less as our sessions continue. Now, we have sessions in which she hardly mentions the assault, and instead dwells on other matters, such as her excitement about her new grandchild.

Nondirective psychotherapy

Nondirective psychotherapy is a form of "talk therapy." The client talks about whatever topic he wants to talk about, for the most part, and the therapist asks questions meant to help the client better feel his feelings. This helps the client deepen his relationship with the therapist. The client can repeat himself about anything as much as he wants, and he can go off on tangents as much as he wants, because every repetition and tangent reveals new perspectives and information.

All the client has to do is adhere to what psychotherapists call the "frame" of the therapy, which means coming for the 50 minute "hour" of therapy, arriving on time, leaving at 10 minutes before the hour, calling ahead to cancel if necessary, and not expecting therapy on an "as needed" basis.

Nondirective psychotherapy works by allowing the client to have a relationship with the therapist that can be called "reparenting." It works by giving the client the attention and interest she has (usually) never had—at least in a non-sexual way. It works by letting the client talk about her life in the presence of an involved other. It works by letting the client attach to someone who is always there, always interested, and able to set limits that encourage the client to be more self-sufficient and self-regulating. It works by letting the client change her perspective on other people in every session, if she needs to do that. She can see her father as loving and caring one week, cruel and indifferent the next. This ability to change perspectives is very important to a client's understanding of the people in her life.

Nondirective psychotherapy gives survivors of sexual assault a chance to repair the fabric of their selves. By "selves" I mean their personalities, their identities, who they are. This talking about whatever they want to talk about becomes a reweaving of their personality threads—threads that have been torn in the assault. Talk therapy is the only way I know of to accomplish this reweaving. When you have nondirective psychotherapy, you will have someone who is with you in your pain. You will love it. If you don't love it at first, you will come to love it. Trust me, I know.

Realizations

You'll see how you are really living your life, not how you think you're living your life. You'll realize that the therapist knows you, is interested in you, gives you a safe place to return to, can be counted on in a crisis, can be admired, denigrated, misunderstood and even hated, all in the same session, and yet will be there the next session, caring about you. You'll see that the therapist can handle your bad self, your good self, your need to hurt yourself, your hatred of other people, and lots of other things you're afraid of, without batting an eyelash. You'll stop having the following very painful feelings:

- fear there is something intrinsically wrong with you
- fear that you'll never measure up to siblings or anyone else
- a desperate need for acceptance by family members
- fear of being left out of other people's good times
- fear that you have to do better than other people in order to feel you're okay

General improvements

Within a few sessions, the client begins deciding what she thinks, instead of reacting to what others think of her. The client begins taking charge of the relationships in her life instead of allowing others to. The client is able to feel her feelings without censoring them. The client gives herself credit for what she has accomplished, instead of beating herself up for what she still needs to do. The client is able to enjoy her decisions, regardless of how those decisions turn out. The client is able to enjoy other people the way they are, and not for what they have or for what they've accomplished. With all these improvements comes a general feeling of well-being the client has never before experienced.

Specific improvements

Clients form happy, healthy new relationships. I have seen this happen many, many times. Clients find new happiness in existing relationships. The clients start wanting sex again. The clients find healthy ways of self-medicating, such as yoga, gardening, walking, and volunteering with needy kids.

Clients become better able to deal with such PTSD symptoms as flashbacks and nightmares. They find they can manage these symptoms when they occur, and also experience them less and less.

Clients also become better able to deal with their perpetrators. They can be in the same room with them without falling apart emotionally, and sometimes they can even forgive the perpetrator and those who facilitated the perpetrator's abuse.

And I have seen, again and again, clients become able to deal with their mothers. This can mean co-existing with their mothers on a superficial basis or rejecting the mothers completely. In both cases, clients understand why their mothers did what they did. Often, the clients come to realize that their mothers had reasons for acting the way they did (and usually still do). They might have been victims of sexual abuse themselves. They might have grown up in extreme poverty, been rejected by their parents, or been so neglected that they were never able to form bonds with the client at all.

Finally, I see clients move on in their lives. They go on to new challenges, new interests, and new goals, leaving the sexual abuse on the back burners of their lives. They begin making appointments for every other week, then taking breaks that might last a month or more, then coming in to say goodbye. These are always tearful but heartwarming occasions. The clients always say they'll keep in touch, but they never do.

And that's exactly how it's supposed to be.

Other forms of therapy

You might find that other forms of therapy work better for you than nondirective psychotherapy. And that's absolutely fine. You might find that you hate nondirective psychotherapy so much that you just have to find other forms of help. That's absolutely fine, too.

Other forms of therapy you might find useful include cognitive behavioral therapy (CBT), rational emotive behavior therapy, and short-term therapy. You can find plenty of information about them on the Internet. For those interested, I've included the two most popular CBT self-help manuals in the "Recommended Reading" section.

Psychiatric medications

Please, don't think I'm a doctor. I am not. I cannot prescribe psychiatric medications and I'm really glad I can't. Only your psychiatrist (or other mental health professional authorized to write prescriptions) can decide what medication is best for you. But I have observed the effects of various psychiatric medications on my clients, and that's what I want to share with you. The more you know about psychiatric drugs, the better off you will be.

Far from all clients need psychiatric medications. The psychotherapy process can often do as much or more good than a medication, even for very disturbed clients. Clients who come to therapy feeling so anxious, depressed, worried, furious, and scared that they can't stand it, usually feel much calmer, more centered, relieved, and hopeful within a few sessions, and can go on with their lives. If this change doesn't happen, then psychiatric medications should be considered.

Many people live their whole lives on meds because they need to, and the quality of their lives is much better as a result.

Several types of psychiatric medication can be helpful to sexual abuse survivors. They include anti-anxiety drugs (such as Ativan), anti-psychotics (such as lithium), opiate blockers (such as Naltrexone—for self-mutilators), and, most importantly, anti-depressants (such as Prozac). These are the type generally of most use to incest and sexual assault survivors. They affect your mood by changing your brain's chemistry. They rearrange the neurotransmitters' output of brain chemicals so that depressed, anxious, and frightened people often become happier, calmer, and better able to deal with their fears.

The effects of anti-depressants vary from person to person. I have seen one patient become absolutely ecstatic on a medication that did not help another at all. Sometimes a psychiatric drug will improve a client's clarity of thought but not his mood, or vice versa.

But there are disadvantages to anti-depressants. Sometimes, they suddenly stop working. The client will keep on taking his medication, but relapse into bouts of weeping, rage, deep depression, or other symptoms. In such cases, the dosage needs to be increased or the medication needs to be augmented by another kind that works on a different brain chemical. But these things don't always work, and even when they do, experimentation with different medications is often needed before an effective combination is found.

When meds fail, the client feels very let down, and also very frightened. What if he can't count on anything helping for very long? At that point, all the assurances I can give fall on deaf ears. I have to let the client suffer his disappointment, because I can't make him feel better anytime soon.

And I have to let the client process the fear that he can't feel good on his own, without meds. "I'm only good if I take those pills," one client said sadly. "And now they're not working anymore! What am I going to do?" This client was not only angry about taking the pills, but he was angry with me and the whole psychotherapy process. The "talk therapy" he'd done was meaningless to him, because the pills had stopped working.

This client is not taking any medications now, and so far he's doing all right—at least he's not doing any worse than he was. In one sense he's doing a lot better than he was, because he now feels that he's taking charge of himself, and that has given him a sense of empowerment he enjoys. And he's more responsive to therapy than he was when he was taking the psychiatric drugs.

What to keep in mind

You should listen to no one but a prescribing medical doctor, nurse practitioner, or psychiatrist about the psychiatric medications you might need. Your therapist can advise and report symptoms to your physician, but he or she should never be in conflict with that professional. The therapist should call the physician and report symptoms that the physician should know about.

Not taking medications, if your doctor says you should, can be dangerous. You could deteriorate to the point where you might commit suicide or try to harm others, such as your children.

You must report every unwanted symptom you experience when you are taking psychiatric medications. A sense of doom, disinterest in life, or a feeling of being too happy or too euphoric to function is cause for alarm. You should tell your therapist and/or physician about these symptoms immediately.

Finally, you must allow the meds enough time to work. Don't stop taking them because you aren't seeing a change. Some clients take their medications so long before the meds "kick in" that they actually can't figure out why their mood is improving when it finally does.

On the other hand, some clients see results in just a few weeks.

The best medications effect I know of

The client (not one of mine) was a flight attendant who had a one-year-old daughter for whom she felt nothing. She had to be away on her job for days at a time and had enough trouble, she said, handling her job, let alone a child. She found herself wishing that she could let someone else raise her daughter, so she wouldn't have to feel guilty about the child all the time.

Then her doctor prescribed Prozac. Within a few months, this woman had changed her attitude toward her daughter completely. Her feelings of love for the child blossomed, and she couldn't wait to be with the little girl. She began calling the child on the phone whenever she had a chance, and upon returning home was flooded with joy at the sight of her.

This medication made it possible for a child to have the mother she needed. There's no better outcome than that.

When you absolutely must consult a professional about taking psychiatric medications, no question about it

- You hear voices that tell you things
- You are sure there is a conspiracy out to get you
- You are in frequent communication with extraterrestrials, demons, fairies, spirits, or other kinds of entities
- You really want to harm yourself
- You repeatedly try to harm yourself
- You can't leave your home, not even to go to the store or to keep a doctor's appointment
- You obsessively spend, eat, gamble, telephone, take in stray cats, or compulsively do anything else that is hurting you and your family
- Your house is such a health hazard that you can't allow anyone to see it because you can't clean it in a reasonable time and/or you have too many pets living there.

If you have any of these symptoms, you might be psychotic. Don't worry about it; it's no reflection on you. You can live a very good life with psychosis—but you have to take your medications. If you don't, you could do major damage to yourself or others, because your reasoning will be seriously impaired.

How do you feel about all this information?

Confused? That's understandable. This information on psychiatric medications was not meant to tell you, "Yes, you should take psychiatric drugs" or "No, you should not take psychiatric drugs." Its purpose was to tell you all I know about how psychiatric drugs can work and maybe can't work, when they are needed, and when they may not be needed. It was also meant to show you there are no hard and fast rules about taking these medications—unless you are having symptoms of psychosis.

But we are lucky to have these drugs if we need them. We should all be able to rely on them when necessary.

B

Recommended Reading and Viewing

Books

Courage to Heal: A Guide for Women Survivors of Child Sexual Abuse (Third Edition), by Ellen Bass and Laura Davis. (Harper and Collins, 1988)

This is the bible of incest survivors. It is indeed good, except for the material on the role of the mother in incest. That part is confusing, ambivalent, and dangerous because it refuses to help you take a stand on your mother's role and hints that no matter what your mother did, she probably meant well and you should forgive her.

Trauma and Recovery, by Judith Lewis Herman, M.D. (Basic Books, 1992)

I love the way this book points out, in the chapter "A Forgotten History," that sexual trauma for women was not considered to exist until Freud's patients revealed it so blatantly that he could not ignore it. But then, thanks to the scorn of his colleagues, even Freud had to claim he was mistaken about it. The author says that if it weren't for combat veterans returning with "shell shock" from World Wars I & II, the symptoms of trauma—flashbacks, nightmares and inability to concentrate, among others—probably never would have been acknowledged. I find the explanations of dissociation and other symptoms in Part I very clear and helpful. Part II deals with recovery and seems to be a little too structured. I do not, as the author seems to, believe that recovery happens in defined stages. I find that it progresses with setbacks, relapses, and resistances in a forward-moving direction if the client keeps coming back, is not using addictive drugs, and the therapist never gives up.

The Body Remembers: The Psychophysiology of Trauma and Trauma Treatment, by Babette Rothschild. (Norton, 2000)

This book explains in mechanical detail why flashbacks, dissociation, panic attacks, irrational fears, and other symptoms of post traumatic stress disorder can come flooding in on a survivor at any time without warning, in the middle of a business presentation or in bed, and the exercises it provides for dealing with these symptoms are clear and simple to carry out.

Treating the Adult Survivor of Childhood Sexual Assault: A Psychoanalytic Perspective, by Jody Messler-Davies and Mary Gail Frawley. (Basic Books, 1994)

A classic text for therapists, but also supremely useful for those survivors willing to read it. This book is difficult, but is very insightful about psychotherapy methods for sexual abuse survivors. If you really want to know how psychotherapy works, please read this book.

Feeling Good: The New Mood Therapy (Revised Edition), by David Burns. (Avon, 1999)

The all-time best-selling self-help book. It takes a cognitive-behavioral approach, and is well written and easy to use.

The Feeling Good Handbook (Revised Edition), by David Burns. (Plume, 1999)

The companion workbook to *Feeling Good*. It contains a myriad of useful self-help exercises.

The Gift of Fear: Survival Signals that Protect Us from Violence, by Gavin de Becker. (Little, Brown & Co., 1997)

An eye-opening guide on how to spot predators, their ploys, and verbal snares, and how to protect yourself against them.

Overcoming Your Alcohol, Drug and Recovery Habits: An Empowering Alternative to AA and 12-step Treatment, by James DeSena. (See Sharp Press, 2003)

A cognitive-behavioral self-help book on overcoming addictions. It contains a useful, detailed section on getting out of abusive situations.

Alcohol: How to Give It Up and Be Glad You Did, by Philip Tate. (See Sharp Press, 1996)

A standard rational emotive behavior therapy (REBT) self-help work on overcoming addictions. Endorsed by and widely used in SMART Recovery.

When AA Doesn't Work for You: Rational Steps to Quitting Alcohol, by Albert Ellis and Emmett Velten. (Barricade Books, 1992)

A standard, very useful work on overcoming addictions by two prominent REBT pscyhologists.

Films

I found the following films to be harrowing but very important validations of the effects of abuse and sexual trauma.

Twist of Faith. Documentary, directed by Kirby Dick. (2004)

This incredibly powerful film includes a scene showing a mother telling her son she is not going to support him and is siding with his molesters. The survivor is Tony Comes, a 33-year-old firefighter in Toledo who was abused by a priest when he was a child. He is fine, or thinks he is fine, until the priest who abused him buys a house five doors down from his. The film begins at that point, and we see Comes' symptoms re-emerge and his life change dramatically for the worse. When he visits his mother to tell her how he feels about the church that allowed his abuse, his mother tells him not to put down the church, that it is her church, and that he is bad for denigrating it. It's very painful watching her place the church that enabled the abuse of her son over her son's welfare.

Mysterious Skin (2004)

This fictional film is about two boys who are molested by a trusted coach. It shows how one becomes a male prostitute and the other becomes a victim of repressed memories that he knows are there, but believes are the result of a UFO abduction. This film is so true in its depictions of these effects it leaves one gasping for breath.